THE LONELIEST BOY IN THE WORLD
The Last Child of the Great Blasket Island

D0054398

GEARÓID CHEAIST Ó CATHÁIN is the only survivor of the islanders evacuated from the Great Blasket. He moved with his parents to Dunquin and was educated at St Joseph's College, Kilkenny, Dingle CBS and School of Commerce, Cork. He enjoyed a varied career and lives in Cork, promoting Irish and occasionally lecturing at University College Cork.

PATRICIA AHERN is co-author of *In Search of the Missing* and *The Lightkeeper*. From Mallow, she lives in County Cork and is currently co-writing a memoir with the renowned traditional singer Seán Ó Sé.

In memory of my grandparents, Ceaist and June Eoghain Bháin and Maras Mhuiris Ó Catháin and Kate Sheáin Mhicíl, and my parents, Seán Cheaist Ó Catháin and Bídí Mharas Mhuiris. Also to my wife Marie, son Graham and daughter Sandra. And most of all to *Muintir an 'Leáin*, the people of the island. But for them, this would never have happened.

THE LONELIEST BOY IN THE WORLD

The Last Child of the Great Blasket Island

GEARÓID CHEAIST Ó CATHÁIN
WITH PATRICIA AHERN

The Collins Press

FIRST PUBLISHED IN 2014 BY
The Collins Press
West Link Park
Doughcloyne
Wilton
Cork

© Gearóid Cheaist Ó Catháin and Patricia Ahern 2014
Reprinted in 2023

Gearóid Cheaist Ó Catháin and Patricia Ahern have asserted their
moral right to be identiFied as the authors of this work in accordance
with the Copyright and Related Rights Act 2000.

All rights reserved.
THe material in this publication is protected by copyright law.
Except as may be permitted by law, no part of the material may be
reproduced (including by storage in a retrieval system) or
transmitted in any form or by any means, adapted, rented or lent
without the written permission of the copyright owners.
Applications for permissions should be addressed to the publisher.

A CIP record for this book is available from the British Library.

Paperback ISBN: 978-1-84889-207-1
PDF eBook ISBN: 978-1-84889-865-3
EPUB eBook ISBN: 978-1-84889-866-0
Kindle ISBN: 978-1-84889-867-7

Images courtesy of the Blasket Centre Archive/Cartlann Ionaid an
Bhlascaoid: pages 4, 9, 11, 22, 42, 49, 51, 56, 65, 67, 69, 71, 73,
77, 82, 84, 95, 98, 101, 103, 118, 146, 156, 201.

Typesetting by Carrigboy Typesetting Services
in Garamond Premier Pro 12pt/14.5pt
Printed in India by Replika Press Pvt. Ltd.

MIX
Paper from
responsible sources
FSC® C016779

Contents

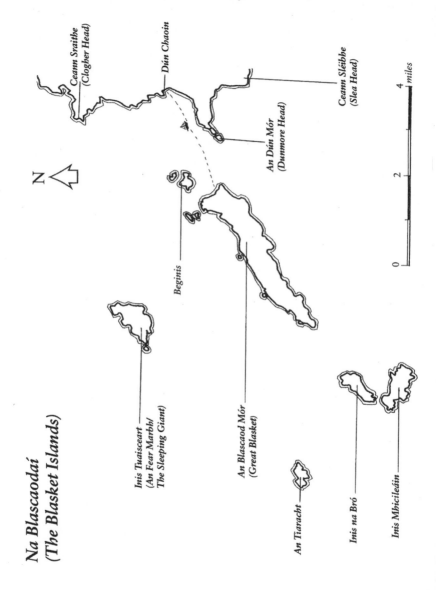

Na Blascaodaí
(The Blasket Islands)

N

Ceann Sratithe
(Clogher Head)

Dún Chaoin

Ceann Sléibhe
(Slea Head)

An Dún Mór
(Dunmore Head)

Beginis

Inis Tuaisceart
(An Fear Marbh/
The Sleeping Giant)

An Blascaod Mór
(Great Blasket)

An Tiaracht

Inis na Bró

Inis Mhicileáin

0   2   4   miles

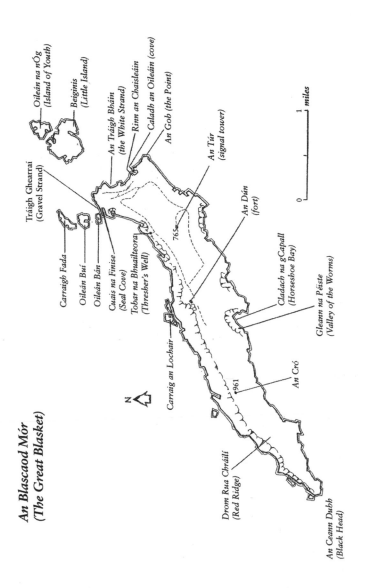

An Blascaod Mór
(The Great Blasket)

Oileán na nÓg (Island of Youth)
Beiginis (Little Island)
An Tráigh Bhán (the White Strand)
Rinn an Chaisleáin
Caladh an Oileáin (cove)
An Gob (the Point)
An Túr (signal tower)
An Dún (fort)
Tráigh Ghearraí (Gravel Strand)
Carraigh Fada
Oileán Buí
Oileán Bán
Cuais na Finise (Seal Cove)
Tobar na Bhuailteora (Thresher's Well)
765n
Cladach na gCapall (Horseshoe Bay)
Gleann na Péiste (Valley of the Worms)
Carraig an Lochair
An Cró
961
Drom Rua Chráilí (Red Ridge)
An Ceann Dubh (Black Head)
N
1 miles
0

I have written minutely of much that we did, for it was my wish that somewhere there should be a memorial of it all, and I have done my best to set down the character of the people about me so that some record of us might live after us, for the like of us will never be again.

TOMÁS Ó CRIOMHTHAIN

Foreword

THE GREAT BLASKET ISLAND was recognised as a bastion of Irish language and culture into the twentieth century and is known for having produced a sizeable body of autobiographical works describing the way of life on the island. Anyone who has had the opportunity to visit the island will note that despite the wild beauty of the landscape, it is indeed a harsh and unforgiving site. Unsheltered and at the mercy of the Atlantic Ocean, not a single tree grows on the island. Islanders traditionally lived a subsistence lifestyle and depended almost entirely on fishing to eke out a living.

Although only a small community, the inhabitants of this little island three miles off the tip of the Dingle Peninsula had a profound effect on modern Irish literature. Not only did the islanders themselves produce some of the greatest pieces of twentieth-century Irish literature, but the Blaskets also attracted linguists and scholars from around the globe.

Poverty and increasing food shortages made the Great Blasket Island uninhabitable and by 1953 Éamon de Valera's government finally gave the order to evacuate the island. By 1954 all remaining inhabitants had been relocated to the mainland. Like many others, Gearóid's family settled in Dún Chaoin. The demise of the island and the evacuation of its residents to the mainland saw a unique culture and community pass into history.

Many of the folk memories and customs remain in the possession of one particular islander: Gearóid Cheaist Ó Catháin. Gearóid was the last child of the Blasket Islands. In fact, of the thirty remaining inhabitants, Gearóid was the only child. In a 1949 newspaper article by Liam Robinson he was described as 'the loneliest boy in the world – he has only seagulls as playmates'. Robinson and a features photographer, Donal MacMonagle, visited Gearóid's family and the other islanders just before Christmas. They wanted to document young Gearóid's story. The poignant story of the only child living on a nearly deserted island captured the hearts and minds of people around the world. What followed was a slew of gifts, money and even the offer of land in Texas to the youngest Blasket islander.

Despite public perception, Gearóid had a wonder-fully happy childhood, cherished and adored by parents and neighbours alike. Moulded by the island's ageing population, he became an heir to a civilisation and island home that were soon to pass; a link between a way of life described by Peig Sayers and Tomás Ó Criomhthain and modern Ireland. Gearóid's own memories are entwined with the beliefs and customs handed down to him by his ancestors. His knowledge provides a valuable insight into twentieth-century life on the Blaskets. He holds a deep connection to a culture that now only survives in literary and historical record.

This book also documents Gearóid's formative years in Dún Chaoin after the islanders' exodus to the mainland and explores his experience of Gaeltacht life. In the Dún Chaoin community, a young Gearóid could pursue a rich and vibrant lifestyle, engaging in Gaelic football and traditional music and even attending formal schooling for the first time. Dún Chaoin was a hub of Irish language learning in the 1950s and 1960s and young Gearóid met people such as the poet Seán O'Ríordáin and actress Siobhán McKenna. This book also explores Gearóid's journey into adulthood and examines the way in which his perspective and personality have been formed by his roots and upbringing.

Through the recollection of Gearóid's earliest memories, we can explore the diverse customs and beliefs of the Blasket Island community until the necessary evacuation of its remaining population. Gearóid's story is a key link to one of the most culturally revered communities in Ireland. He belongs to the island's final generation and therefore much of the island's culture and history remain in his possession. We are privileged to relive the last days of life on the Blasket Islands in his company. Gearóid invites us onto the island to meet the last inhabitants of the Blasket community and he recounts the events and people that shaped his childhood. He looks back with kindness and humility on the elders who shielded him from the hardship of island life while also bestowing upon him the gifts of folklore, music and tradition. His family's connection to traditional music was of particular importance to him; his father, a noted fiddler, is associated with the haunting air '*Port na bPúcaí*'.

Gearóid's memories are interwoven with those of his ancestors and he speaks with authority on their behalf while he recounts the difficulties and challenges that faced final generations on the island. In essence, Gearóid's is indeed a personal story, but his biography also documents a time of great change in the history and culture of the communities to which he belonged.

I once asked Gearóid about how his upbringing had influenced his perspective on life. He described himself as an *oileánach i measc slua* – an islander amongst the crowd. I feel this perfectly captures the poignancy of Gearóid's unique situation: the last-born child of an island community that is no more.

The Blasket islanders may have come to pass, but their memories live on in the hearts and minds of many. Life on the Blaskets may be a thing of the past, but thanks to people like Gearóid, the memories will live on. The often-quoted '*Ní bheidh ár leithéidí arís ann*' seems a fitting epitaph for a community and a way of life of which nothing remains but crumbling cottages, windswept wilderness and, of course, the invaluable memories of the last child of the Blasket Islands.

FIONA CROWE BA, MA
Fiona and Gearóid met in 2006 when they worked together at Gael Taca.

Prologue

THE YOUNGER MEN, like Faeilí and his brother, seemed to want to go. But the older men, most of whom had spent all their life on the island, were non-committal. A common saying on the island was, 'It's God's will.' And that seemed to be their attitude. They took life a day at a time, in whatever shape or form it came, and never complained. They put up no argument and made no drama about leaving. My grandfather Ceaist made no comment whatsoever. There was a certain calmness about it all.

Somehow, I sensed my mother wanted to go. In recent months, she had seemed restless and had begun to spend more and more time on the mainland with her sister Kate, who lived in Beenbawn, outside Dingle, and with her sister Lís, who lived in Graffies, near the village of Feothanach. When she visited them she always took me with her, which meant I was also spending less time on the island.

When she was at home, she whiled away a lot of the day with her mother or Mary Pheats Mhicí, one of the women on the island. She must have found the summer days especially long and lonely, as my father would have been gone from dawn to dusk.

She was also becoming more concerned about my schooling, as I was nearly six years of age. Making sure I got an education became her priority.

But I think she'd had enough of island life by then and longed to move away from its severity and isolation and live in cosier conditions. Being a young woman, still only in her thirties, she must have craved the company of people her own age.

PART 1

1

The Child

NO MATTER HOW far in life we travel, we can never shake off our roots. That's why the Blasket Islands are still a part of me. They hold a special place in my heart and I can't let go.

The Blasket Islands are a cluster of islands and rocks huddled together off County Kerry, on the southwest coast of Ireland, in the Irish-speaking parish of Dunquin. The main islands are An Blascaod, Beginis, Inis na Bró, Inis Tuaisceart, An Tiaracht and Inis Mhicileáin. Even the sound of their names is music to my ears.

Like generations of my ancestors, I am a native of the biggest island, An Blascaod Mór, or the Great Blasket. The name Blascaod may come from the Norse word *brasker*, which means a sharp reef and describes the island well, or it may originate from the Irish word *blaosc,* meaning shell.

Facing the top of the Great Blasket from the commonage with An Tráigh Bháin below to the right. The islanders sowed potatoes in the fields every spring, turning over every sod with a spade.

When I lived on the Great Blasket, from the time of my birth to the age of six, I was the only child there. I left in 1953, when the island was evacuated. Of the evacuated islanders, I am now the only survivor.

Being a native islander and the only child on the island has left its mark on me. In a crowd, even among only three people, I feel uneasy. I am happiest of all when I am alone. I crave isolation and peace.

The Great Blasket stretches on the Atlantic Ocean like a giant humpbacked whale, over three miles long and less than two miles wide, with the smaller Blasket

Islands scattered close by, as if paying homage. Most of the island is hilly and its backbone edge drops sharply down to the sea, with barely a square yard of even ground to be seen apart from a few small headlands, its narrow cliff top and the dunes behind the strand, which was once a popular place for dancing. The village lies at the eastern end of the island, facing the mainland, and nestles in under the side of the hill. A web of pathways runs from house to house, often in a zigzag way, showing the close ties between the people of the Great Blasket, who were always over and back, up and down, visiting each other.

The view from its highest point, An Cró, with a peak of 961 feet, is breathtaking. The tiny, flat island of Beginis lies below, while the nearest village, Dunquin, can be seen resting on the tip of the Dingle Peninsula. Dunmore Head sits in the distance and the famous Skellig Michael stands proud, with its lighthouse and pointed rocks reaching high up to the sky. Inis Tuaisceart lies north of the other islands as well as An Tiaracht, the most westerly of them all, a jagged pyramid of rock and home to another lighthouse, with Slea Head close by. Further on, the outlines of Portmagee and Ballinskelligs can be seen, while south of An Cró lies Inis na Bró and Inis Mhicileáin, an island made famous by its owner, the late Charles Haughey. My father, Seán Cheaist Ó Catháin, used to say that if you climbed to the top of An Cró on a clear day, you could see the west coast of Clare.

Even though the people on the mainland lived only three miles across the sea and spoke in Irish like the people of the Great Blasket, the islanders were different, a people apart. We were a small, isolated fishing community, the most westerly settlement in Europe. The island had no doctor, priest, school or church and no electricity or running water. In many ways, we were self-sufficient. But we were also vulnerable. Living on a barren, windswept island, we were open to the elements of nature and constantly battled against them for survival. When the sun shone on the Great Blasket it was heaven, with a cloudless, turquoise sky above, glistening waves swishing in rhythm below on the white strand, which we called An Tráigh Bháin, and thousands of colourful birds happily twittering and tweeting. But when the weather took a turn for the worse and imprisoned us, it was hell, with a ferocious, rolling sea battering the rocks, constantly venting its anger against the island and its people and relentlessly shooting sea spray thirty feet into the air. If medical help was needed when the island was cut off from the mainland by storm, an improvement in the weather could mean the difference between life and death.

When I lived on the Great Blasket, the nearest to me in age was my mother's brother, Maraisín Mhuiris, who was thirty years older than me. But I never took any notice of being the only child on the island, as I felt that the rest of the islanders were as young as me and that I was as old as them. Even when children visited the island, it made little difference to me. I was happy as I was. I loved everyone around me and felt that they loved me too, as they always had great time for me and took pleasure in all I did. When they spoke about me without using my name, they referred to me simply as *an leanbh*, which means the child.

Like me, my mother, who was known as Bídí Mharas Mhuiris, held a unique place on the island. She was the only young married woman there, as all the other young female islanders had moved to the mainland in search of a better life or had emigrated, mainly to the railway town of Springfield, Massachusetts, in America, often called the next parish west. Understandably, when my mother became pregnant during her first year of marriage, there was great excitement on the island.

On 21 July 1947, I was born in Saint Elizabeth's hospital in Dingle, which was the nearest market town. My mother, who was thirty-two years of age then, decided to give birth on the mainland even though many children had been safely delivered on the island in earlier times with the help of Méiní, a nurse and midwife who had lived on the island for thirty-six years. Her real name was Máire Ní Shé and she was related to my family through marriage, as a relative of mine named Seán Bhailt Ó Catháin was married to Máire's sister. At the time of the marriage, the bride was only fourteen years of age.

A local priest and Debbie Donaghue, whom my mother had chosen to be my godmother, came to the hospital for my baptism. But it had to be postponed because my father and my mother's brother, Seán Mharas Mhuiris Ó Catháin, who was known as Faeilí, failed to turn up on the day. Once they set foot on the mainland, instead of going straight to the hospital, they made themselves snug in a pub, drank too much and ended up staying the night in Dingle at the house of my mother's cousins.

The next day, I was christened Gearóid Cheaist Ó Catháin. The name Ceast comes from the word *ceast*, which is a heavy stone or lump of iron, and was used to distinguish our family from others of the same surname. It originated at a time when my paternal grandfather, Pádraig Ó Catháin, proved himself to be the best at rock throwing, which was a popular pastime with the men of the island when they gathered on the flat of the Great Blasket's main path above the strand, An Tráigh Bháin. From then on, my grandfather was called Ceaist.

By coincidence, my mother's maiden name was also Ó Catháin, but her family and my father's were not related. When my father wrote an official letter or a letter to his aunts, uncles or cousins in America, he used the English version of our surname, which was Keane, while my mother's family used the English surname Kane.

The Child

Gearóid and his parents outside their home on the island.

When I was six days old, my parents and I set out on our journey home to the Great Blasket. We took a taxi from the hospital to Dunquin, which was a fourteen-mile trip, and then rowed three miles to the island in a *naomhóg*, which is a special type of currach. My father and Faeilí as well as our neighbour Seán Mhaidhc Léan Ó Guithín worked the oars.

When we landed at the slipway of the Great Blasket, all the islanders had gathered. One by one, they greeted us and showered us with their blessings. As my mother made her way up the rocky pathway from the landing, cradling me in her arms, everyone followed and went to the home of my father's parents, which my parents and grandparents shared. There the celebrations began in earnest, with plenty to eat and drink and much singing, music, dancing, storytelling and smoking.

My homecoming was deemed a great occasion, as new life had been injected into a dying community crushed by emigration. While my parents and grand-parents must have been proud on the day, they must also have wondered what lay ahead for me, as there was no other child in sight as a playmate for me or a school in which to educate me. Yet as the ageing community raised their glasses of whiskey, stout and sherry to toast my health and happiness and that of my family, nobody could have imagined that in only a few years, I would become famous worldwide and that the isolated Great Blasket would become known all around the globe.

With my arrival, the island now had about thirty inhabitants. It was divided into two sections, Bun a' Bhaile and Barr a' Bhaile. We lived in the lower section, Bun a' Bhaile, just above the boat landing, from which a pathway ran, known as Bóithrín na Marbh, meaning road of the dead. Its name originated from the fact that the deceased of the island were shouldered along that trail to the slipway on their way for burial on the mainland, usually in Dunquin or Ventry. The houses were scattered here and there, one above the other, each bedded into its own little hollow.

Our house was perched in a field to the left of the pathway and overlooked the quay. Peaidí Mharas Ó

(*L–r*): Maras Mhaidhc Léan, Gearóid, Mary Pheats Mhicí
Uí Guithín and Seán Mhaidhc Léan. Photo: Risteárd
Ó Glaisne.

Dálaigh and his sons Peaidí Beag and Tom Pheaidí
Mharas lived behind us, as well as Seán Mhicil Ó
Súilleabháin, his wife June Mháire Eoghain and their
sons Seánín Mhicil, Peaidí Mhicil and Maidhc Mhicil,
all known as the Micilí. Seán Kearney, who was known

as Seán Sheáisí, and his mother Lís lived across the way in the post office. Seán Kearney, the postman, who was known as Seán Fillí, lived nearby, as did Séamus Mhéiní, Muiris Ó Duinnshléibhe, who was known as Muiris Mór, and Maidhc Faight with his sister Mary.

Higher up the pathway, at Barr a' Bhaile, a widower named Eoghan Sheáin Eoghain Ó Duinnshléibhe, whom we called Tiúit, lived alone. He was a step-brother to Muiris Mór. Seán Tom Kearney, another widower, lived beside the old school, which had closed in 1941, while Maras Mhuiris Ó Catháin and his wife Kate Sheáin Mhichíl, my maternal grandparents, lived above him, along with their sons Faeilí, Peaidí Mhuiris and Maraisín Mhuiris. Sadly, my uncle Peaidí Mhuiris died of illness the following year. He had been in the army before I was born, as had Maraisín Mhuiris. Behind my grandparents' home stood the house of Mary Pheats Mhicí Uí Guithín, who was a widow, and her sons Seán Mhaidhc Léan and Maras Mhaidhc Léan, with the home of Peats Shéamais nearby. Pádraig Mistéal, my granduncle, came and went, as he was a rover and spent much time in America and Canada as well as at Carhue in Dunquin, with relatives.

At its peak, the island had boasted about two hundred inhabitants. Now, in between the occupied dwellings lay many deserted houses, some of which were used as outhouses while others stood in ruins. Our house had been built by my grandfather Ceaist. When he married my grandmother, June Eoghain

Gearóid on top of the slipway on the Great Blasket.
Courtesy of Donal MacMonagle/macmonagle.com

Bháin, also a native of the Great Blasket, he was
working as a fisherman in Dingle and had no land of his
own, while his parents still lived on the Great Blasket.
After marrying, my grandparents lived in Dingle over

a pub owned by a man called Tobac. Being poor, my grandfather paid the rent by playing his fiddle in the pub. My grandparents stayed over the pub until my grandmother's father, Eoghan Bán, offered them a field on the Great Blasket, in which an old Protestant church was located. My grandfather built a house in that field, which became my home too. It was made of mortar and clay and roofed with canvas, wood and felt, which was later coated in tar. It had one chimney.

I remember the house well. Its front porch stored buckets of water from the well, Tobar na Croise, which was located between our house and the sea-shore and got its name from an old stone cross that had once stood above the well. The house had two small windows, one in the kitchen and one in the bedroom, and a back door. The kitchen was big, with a fine hearth. It burned all day, every day, summer and winter, as it was used not only for heat but also for cooking. The ground around the fire was flagstone, while the rest of the kitchen floor was covered in hard earth. Beside the hearth stood six big ornamental glass wine casks. My grandfather Ceaist had got them from foreign fishermen in exchange for inshore fish, which they considered a delicacy. He was great at bartering, especially with French and Spanish trawlermen. The focal point of the room was a dresser, which was my mother's pride and joy. It displayed her fancy, colourful ware, all shining and neatly arranged, with some plates standing on their sides to show off their flowery pattern and china cups dangling on hooks.

My father, a fisherman, was gifted with his hands. He made shoes and many of the islanders relied on him for a good haircut. He crafted a beautiful wooden statue of the Blessed Virgin Mary, which he painted in blue and white and etched with the letters BVM. It stood in a glass case that hung on the kitchen wall. He made most of the kitchen furniture, including a wooden table, which stood beside the fire. He also crafted a long wooden stool and three *súgán* chairs, which had roped seating and backs, as well as a small stool for me. We had an old high-backed wooden chair from a shipwreck, with bolts, as it had been bolted onto the deck of the ship. A narrow moveable panel divided the bedroom, which was shared by my grandparents, my parents and me. For light we used a paraffin oil lamp, unlike the middle classes in Dunquin, who burned methylated spirits in Tilley lamps.

We kept chickens in a lean-to at the back of our house. Beside the house stood an old deserted house that we used as an outhouse to store wooden barrels of salted fish, mainly mackerel, wrasse, conor and ling, all layered and coated in coarse salt. The house had once belonged to my father's cousins, who had lived there until they emigrated to America. In another outhouse further away, we housed a cow and a donkey.

Until I reached the age of one, our house was quiet, so my mother used to say. Soon afterwards, all hell broke loose.

On Christmas Eve 1948, a journalist named Liam Robinson and a features photographer called Donal

Gearóid's grandfather Pádraig (Ceaist) Ó Catháin and
Gearóid at Bun a' Bhaile on the Great Blasket.

MacMonagle climbed up the steep path from the
slipway carrying parcels, meal, a crate of stout and two
bottles of Parliament whiskey. They had come to the
Great Blasket for a three-day visit and stayed in the
house of Mary Pheats Mhicí, who often kept tourists.
Mary, a tall, slender woman, was a daughter of Pádraig
Ó Catháin, or Peats Mhicí, as he was called. During
his lifetime he was known as the king, an honorary
title given to him by the islanders due to his regal
appearance, wisdom and strength.

The two press men roamed all over the island, chatted to the islanders and captured them on camera. They had known that I was the only child on the Great Blasket even before they set foot on the island and came to our house laden with presents for me. My mother got into a fuss and began scrubbing my face, combing my head of curls and straightening out my clothes. The photographer took snapshots of my father, grandfather and me, including one of my father and his fiddle, as he was a fine traditional musician, like his own father, and also played the melodeon.

A photograph of me with my father and his fiddle was published, along with a newspaper article about my life. It carried the headline, 'The Loneliest Boy in the World'. Its sub-headline stated that I had only the seagulls as playmates. The feature was syndicated in different newspapers all over the world, among them the *News of the World* and *The Australian People*. It sparked a trail of publicity and interest in my life and the lives of my parents. The article captured the imagination of readers of many nationalities and touched their hearts. It seemed people completely fell for the notion that I was indeed the loneliest boy in the world.

Overnight, my family and I became famous. An avalanche of post flooded in from all over the globe, mostly from England, America, Australia and New Zealand. Seán Fillí, our postman, who was my father's cousin, had a path worn to our door. Day after day, he'd trudge across from the post office weighed down with a sack full of letters, postcards and parcels of clothes, books, comics and toys. He'd empty his postbag on the kitchen table, turn to my mother and laugh, 'More of the same, Bídí.' Then he'd ruffle my curls and say, 'Gearóid, I think you'll have to open up a toy shop.' And he was right, because soon we could barely walk around the house without tripping over trucks and trains or some newly invented gadget, the likes of which had never been seen before on the Great Blasket. The parcels, letters and postcards kept coming for years. There seemed to be no end to them.

My favourite toy was a big, black, remote-controlled car. I grew dizzy from watching it circling round and round the kitchen, with its red and blue lights flashing. Our big old brown dog, Sheridan, didn't know what to make of it and barked his head off every time I switched it on. I loved a hydraulic turtle too, as it took off with just a squeeze. The picture storybooks and huge comics fuelled my imagination and I flicked through the pages excitedly. If a certain picture took my fancy, I gazed at it forever, flipped through some more pages and went back to it again. I pestered my mother to read to me, as I was unable to read myself. All the writing was in English and Mam translated each word to Irish for me without a bother. She had good English, as she had worked on the mainland for years in places such as Tralee, Limerick and Dublin, mainly as a cook or a priest's housekeeper. She had also worked in Dingle for a Protestant minister named Roycroft. When she read to me, I was blown away by the cowboy stories. Roy Rogers, Davy Crockett, Buck Jones, the Kansas Kid, Buffalo Bill and Wild Bill Hickok all became my heroes. Sometimes I turned a kitchen chair backwards and perched myself on it and pretended to be one of the cowboys in my comics, galloping off into the wild and shooting my gun high into the air. My grandmother, who was a quiet woman, got a great kick out of it. She'd sit by the fire knitting woollen socks or jumpers, with a small shawl over her shoulders, beaming at my playacting. 'Who are you today, Gearóid?' she'd ask. Then she'd rock herself to and fro and laugh heartily at my reply.

Most days, Mam and I strolled up to Barr a' Bhaile to visit Mam's parents. I'd be leaping out of my skin with excitement, impatient to show them my latest toy. As we'd draw near to the cottage, Mam would plead with me to calm down. She'd point her finger at me and warn me not to burst in the door, as my grandfather, who was the oldest man on the island, might be having a snooze or he might be in a cranky mood. But she may as well have been talking to the wall, as I never paid any heed and always raced ahead and charged in the door. My grandfather, who was a small, stooped, blocky man with a big moustache, would often pretend he wanted my new toy to keep for himself. He'd chase me around the kitchen with the hook of his big walking cane stretched out to clutch me. When he'd finally catch me, he'd tickle the daylights out of me until my grandmother would beg him to stop. Then she'd settle her shawl, wave her hand and say to me, 'Come over here, Gearóid, and show me what you've on you today.'

We must have been the best-dressed family on the island because parcels of fine clothes poured in not only for me, but also for my parents. Mam was in her element, dressing me up in all the different outfits and trying to decide which one I should wear each morning. She loved to look well herself too and had a good dress sense. Even before the parcels starting coming, she had never dressed like the older women of the island, who always wore long, dark dresses, black stockings, cross-over aprons and shawls, usually a short one for indoors and a long one for outdoors. Instead, she dressed in the fashion of the day, like the women on the mainland. When she put on a new dress from the parcels for the first time, she'd always ask my father, 'Well, Seán, what do you think?' Then she'd do a twirl and give him a history of the dress, telling the name of the sender and the country it had been posted from.

Sometimes Dad wore a fancy pullover from the parcels, but most of the time he dressed like the other men on the island in a thick, plain, zipped-up jumper and clothes of heavy cloth bought in Dingle or sent by relations in America. To soak up the salt water and cut down on wettings, most of the men wore a one-piece woollen or flannel undergarment, which they called a drawers. Some wore a waistcoat, often made of leather, or a short coat and trousers of heavy woollen material. Many wore oilskins when fishing, but not all the men found them comfortable. They all wore hobnailed boots made especially for them by a cobbler in Dingle. The boots were well crafted, gave good balance and lasted a lifetime, unlike wellingtons, which were made of poor material then and were slippery. All the island men wore peaked tweed caps too, winter and summer, even in sweltering heat. Some tilted the caps to the side, right or left. Others wore them back-to-front or with the fastener open. The style they wore them in often depended on their mood. Dad took off his cap only at meal times and left it on a rung under his chair while he ate.

As well as the parcels, we got bundles of letters, stacks upon stacks of them, with at least two offers of adoption from America. Patrick Fitzgerald, a Minnesota rancher of Irish descent, wrote to ask if he could adopt me, as he and his wife had lost two young children. In time, he said, I would inherit their property. My parents thanked him for his kind offer but said they could not part with me. Mr Fitzgerald wrote again and offered to take all three of us to America, with a promise of work for Mam and Dad. Mam was broad-minded and saw it as a chance for a better life, but Dad refused to go. Mam respected his

Gearóid's favourite uncle Faeilí whose real name was Seán Maras Mhuiris Ó Catháin and who was great fun.

wishes even though she was the boss in the house, as was every other woman on the island.

An English lady named Mrs Shires became Mam's pen pal and sent her a huge portrait of the British royal family, all dressed in marine attire. Alan Thomas

Moore, a medical student from New Zealand, wrote often for years. Mam used to call him my pen pal, as he addressed all his letters to me, even though it was Mam who always replied on my behalf. He wrote about his daily life in Christchurch and he always put in a small toy for me, maybe a gun or a book, usually with pictures of sheep. I grew attached to a brown cuddly bear he once sent. The teddy went to bed with me every night and I snuggled up tight to him for warmth.

Maybe the letters and parcels stretched my imagination somewhat and aroused my curiosity, because by the time I could talk, I had become the most curious child under the sun, or so Mam used to say. Any time I opened my mouth a string of questions flowed out, one after the other. The grown-ups usually gave me short, run-of-the-mill answers, except one of Mam's brothers, my favourite uncle, Faeilí. He was the only one who could shut me up, as he had a wicked imagination and his answers always left me dumbfounded.

Once I asked Faeilí why Tiúit – who was a close friend of my grandfather Ceaist – had a moustache. Faeilí tipped his cap back on his head, raised his eyebrows, folded his arms and said to me, 'Well, Gearóid, I'll tell you this now, but don't tell another soul. Tiúit had a different moustache one time. But one night when he bent down to put a sod of turf in the fire, the flames burned it off. And would you believe it, when he grew a second moustache, it turned out a different colour to the first?'

Another day, when I was sailing in a *naomhóg* to Beginis with Faeilí, my father and Tiúit to shear sheep, I rummaged in Faeilí's sack and found a hammer and a hatchet. When I asked him why he carried them, he winked at me and said, 'Have a look at Tiúit's big ears. Between here and Beginis, I'll ask him a question, which I know he won't be able to answer. Then I'll hop up like a bullet, knock him on the head with my hammer and chop off his two ears with my hatchet.'

As well as having a wild imagination, Faeilí was daring and often acted on impulse. One calm summer's day I went fishing with Faeilí, my father and Maras Mhaidhc Léan Ó Guithín off the west side of the Great Blasket. They baited their nets with crab and fished for pollock, cod, conor and wrasse. As we neared Oileán Buí, which is a bird sanctuary close to Beginis, we noticed a hive of bird activity. Faeilí got a mad notion to raid the seagulls' nests. 'We'll pull in over there, lads,' he said, bursting to go. He stepped out of the boat with his cap in his hand and ran up a steep hill like a young goat. In a matter of minutes he was back in the boat, laughing his head off, with a dozen seagull eggs in his cap. He went into the stern, carefully took out the eggs from his cap and some paper, as many island men stored paper in their caps for lighting their pipes by the fire. At the bow end of the boat he put a piece of paper in the bailing-can, which is a metal buoy cut in half and used to scoop out water, and which we called the *píosa*, then settled the eggs inside. They were specked with blue and grey and looked like free-range eggs, although they were much smaller than hen eggs. When we landed he gave me a few to take home and Mam hard-boiled them on the fire. The yolk was a reddish-yellow colour and the white part was as white as snow. 'I suppose Faeilí has his own eggs well eaten by now,' Mam laughed as she sat down to the table and cracked her egg with a teaspoon.

I spent more time with Faeilí than my father, who was a quiet man. Faeilí was full of fun and never held back if he had anything to say. Like my mother, he was fussy about clothes. In his mind, the island men were properly dressed on a Sunday only if they wore a navy suit. Whenever Faeilí went to the mainland for Mass and spotted an islander in a gaudy outfit, he shouted, 'Did you get that in a parcel from America?'

He had a knack of making me feel useful. When we went to the bog on the hill for turf or to An Tráigh Bháin for sand, he made sure I brought along my small plastic bucket and spade. I put them into the baskets on either side of his donkey and brought them back full to the brim. When he caught rabbits, he threw a few on my back to carry home.

He was a great cook, had a huge appetite and kept a special plate for my use only. He'd pile it up with food and say, 'Now eat up there, Gearóid, and you'll grow up to be a fine man, just like your uncles.'

Eoghan Sheáin Eoghain Ó Duinnshléibhe, who was known
as Tiúit. He was a great boatman and was the best friend
of Gearóid's grandfather Ceaist. Courtesy of the National
Library of Ireland, Colman Doyle Collection.

Tiúit, who had no family of his own and had spent
many years in America, was also kind to me. He often
gave me duck eggs, which were my favourite eggs.

Sometimes I tried to count the number of spots on each one before handing them over to Mam. She cooked them gently, just enough to make them soft and runny. She made sure that I always thanked Tiúit for the duck eggs and warned me to call him by his real name, as nobody dared call him Tiúit to his face.

Tiúit's duck eggs were a treat, but food on the whole was plentiful, as Dad was a great hunter of rabbits, our supply of salted fish lasted right through the winter and we had fresh fish from May to October. To avoid running short of food in times of bad weather, we stocked tea, sugar and flour in big supplies.

For breakfast we always ate a big bowl of porridge made with fresh milk from our one and only cow, which Mam always milked. My mother's father had a cow too, as did Mary Pheats Mhicí, Seán Tom Kearney and Seán Mhicil Ó Súilleabháin, which meant even if one cow was dry the others were likely to be milking, so being without fresh milk was unlikely. But Mam kept a tin of condensed milk too. It was sweeter and thicker than fresh milk and Dad had a liking for it. Sometimes Tiúit arrived with a half-pint stout bottle of creamy goat's milk, which had a yellow-brownish colour. He kept two kid goats as well as a male and a female. By day he tethered them at the side of his house and he brought them inside at night.

We had our own butter too. Mam made it in a rectangular-shaped wooden churn, which had a handle at the side and two spatulas inside. In the evenings she poured milk into bowls to allow the cream to rise to the top. Later, she spooned off the cream and placed it in another bowl, then she poured it into the churn and rotated the handle until the mixture became solid. She strained off the buttermilk into big bowls, took out the butter and used a butter bat to mix in a load of salt, as salt was hugely popular on the Great Blasket. We drank the buttermilk. It had the consistency of melted ice cream and tasted sour. Sometimes Mam used a glass jar to make butter instead of the wooden churn. She simply poured the cream into the jar, corked it and then shook it until the cream hardened.

Mam always served dinner bang on at one o'clock, not a minute later, as she was a dinger on time and organisation. We often ate lamb, pig's feet or pig's head, which hung over the fireplace and was cut into chunks when needed, then boiled in a big pot with turnip. Eggs were part of our daily diet, as we kept about ten chickens. Mam used many of the eggs for baking, especially for white bread, brown bread and maize bread, all of which she baked in a big iron pot.

Although we were well fed all the year round, nothing could beat the supplies we had at Christmas. That was the best time of all. Christmas 1951 stands out in my mind. The build-up started early for me. Weeks before Christmas, Seán Fillí, the postman, drummed up the excitement every time he called by mentioning Santa Claus. He'd tug the peak of his cap and ask, 'Well, Gearóid, what is Santa Claus going to bring you?' Or he might say, 'When is Santa Claus coming?' Then my head would be filled with nothing but thoughts of Santa. Every day, I pranced around Mam and plagued her with questions, asking where exactly on the island Santa would land with his reindeer and would the ground be even enough for a safe landing, as Faeilí said it was too bumpy for a cart and never used a cart with his donkey because of that. And what if it was a foggy night, or stormy? I became breathless asking questions; I couldn't get them out of my mouth fast enough. To put my mind at ease, Seán Tom Kearncy promised to row Santa over from Dunquin, while the Micilí said not to worry as they would have a fine, strong, three-handed, brand new *naomhóg* finished just in time to ferry him across if Seán Tom couldn't make the trip. In between all the madness, Mam made sure I knew the true meaning of Christmas and told me all about the birth of the baby Jesus. But the grown-ups were just as excited as me about Christmas, especially when they spotted Seán Fillí making tracks for their houses, as everyone expected gifts and money at Christmas from relations in America.

About a week before Christmas, Mam set off for Dingle in the morning to collect the Christmas fare. Dad, Faeilí, Seán Mhaidhc Léan Ó Guithín and Seán Fillí ferried her over to Dunquin.

From evening time on, I was like a hen with an egg, dashing in and out to our front door and looking out to sea, waiting for the first glimpse of her return. At dusk, I spotted the boat near Dunmore Head. I shouted to my grandparents that Mam was on her way home and told my grandfather to hurry up and put on his coat. My heart pounded with excitement and I kept my eyes glued to the boat, afraid I might lose sight of it.

My grandfather and I strolled down to the quay hand in hand. Most of the islanders joined us to hear all the news from the mainland and help bring up the parcels. I clutched onto Mam when she stepped out of the boat, which overflowed with her purchases, a keg of stout bought by Faeilí for his own house and the parcels and letters sent by post for the islanders, which Seán Fillí had collected at the post office in Dunquin.

All our parcels were stacked high on the kitchen table, apart from the Christmas toys for me, which were quickly hidden. As Mam reached for the scissors to snip the twine on the packages and spread their contents on the table, I became giddy with anticipation. Soon the table was jam packed with bottles of stout, whiskey, sherry, lemonade, an iced Christmas cake, a fruit cake, a plum pudding and blue, yellow, red, green and white one-foot candles as well as the contents of the posted packages from our relations in America, mostly clothes and pipes for my father, as he was fascinated with pipes, especially Peterson pipes.

On Christmas Eve morning, my grandfather called me early from my bed and we headed off to the strand for a bucket of sand. Mam was busy polishing up the house and arranging the Christmas cards on the windowsills, sweeping the slab stones and throwing fresh sand on the floor. When we got home, Mam and Dad set up the candles. They stood a candle inside a two-pound jam jar, packed the jar with sand and decorated it with Christmas paper. Mam placed the red candle on the kitchen windowsill and scattered the rest all about the house. Then Faeilí strolled in, full of Christmas cheer and bringing bunches of ivy, which he laid around all the pictures on the walls, among them a picture of the Sacred Heart, and over the dresser. We had no holly, as growth on the island was poor due to the salt of the sea spray.

At that time we treated Christmas Eve as a day of fast and abstinence, which meant we ate no meat and ate only at meal times. At dinnertime we sat down to a feed of salted ling, which left us dying of thirst for the rest of the day. For our evening tea we had thick, buttered slices of homemade porter cake, which Mam always kept as a Christmas Eve treat, and hot cocoa.

At dusk, the magic moment arrived. Mam called me and told me it was time to light the candles. Dad settled a chair by the windowsill for me to stand on while Mam struck a match, handed it to me and helped me light each candle. The glow of the candles on the ivy and windows and the flames from the hearth sent magical, flickering shadows across the kitchen and swept me into an enchanted wonderland. I ran around the room from wall to wall, trying to catch the dancing shadows. I knew it would be just as magical outside and I dashed out the front door and looked up in awe at the village, alight with a shimmering candle on every windowsill. A full moon shone over Dunmore Head, lighting up the channel to the Blaskets, and the frosted felt roofs of the houses glistened like crystal. The stillness in the air was palpable. It was a magical night on the island.

Later, Tiúit dropped in and we all sat around the fire. Mam gave the men a bottle of stout. My grandfather smoked his pipe and chewed tobacco. He had a hole in one of his back teeth and always lodged tobacco there, ready to chew. Mam and Dad lit up a Player's cigarette. Dad smoked one of his favourite pipes too and filled it with a new brand of tobacco, which brought a fresh aroma to the house. He owned a huge collection of pipes, most of which came from his first cousin in America, Dan Connor, to whom he wrote often. Then Mam pulled down the fiddles, which always hung over the fire, and my father and grandfather played while Tiúit nodded his head to the beat and my grandmother tapped her feet and sipped a glass of sherry. They started with lively jigs and reels, then slowed down the tempo with a fairy lament, *'Port na bPúcaí'*, or *'Caoineadh na Síóg'*, as it was sometimes called. Some say the sad, haunting air came from Inis Mhicileáin in the eighteenth century, when a fairy woman was overheard singing it as a lament for the death of one of the fairies on the island. Others say it originates from the call of a seal heard at night in a cove on Inis Mhicileáin. Most feel it echoes the swish of the sea and evokes images of waves thrashing against the cliffs. In between tunes, Dad switched over to the melodeon. When Mam spotted me rubbing my eyes she said it was time for me to hit the hay, as Santa had left the North Pole and would soon be flying over Bantry Bay.

On Christmas morning I stood in front of the kitchen table, mesmerised by the stack of presents from Santa, not knowing which to open first. My favourite gift was a drum. That was the best present ever. I paraded around the village for hours, up and down between Bun a' Bhaile and Barr a' Bhaile, banging the drum as loud as I could, with a pair of blue sandals from America on my feet and a new peaked black and white cardboard cap on my head with the royal insignia in the centre. Dad had made the cap especially for me for Christmas, as he knew I had taken a shine to the peaked caps in the royal portrait sent by Mrs Shires. I drove all the dogs in the village wild with my drum and they waddled along beside me, barking with all their might. Any time Tiúit saw me having fun, he always egged me on. When he heard all the commotion as I strutted up the pathway to Barr a' Bhaile, he appeared at his front door, waved his cap in the air and shouted, 'Louder, Gearóid, louder, so they'll hear you across the water in Dunquin!' When Faeilí saw me coming, he ran ahead of me and marched on for a few hundred yards, swinging a big stick in the air, pretending he was leading a band.

For Christmas dinner we had a leg of lamb, as Faeilí killed a sheep every Christmas and divided it out among the islanders. Then we tucked into Mam's homemade plum pudding and later some apples and oranges, which were a rarity in our house at other times of the year.

In the evening, Mam and I strolled up the hill to Barr a' Bhaile to visit her parents and brothers. My grandfather Maras Mhuiris pressed some coins into my hand, as he always gave me money on Christmas Day. Then he cut some tasty homemade maize bread into different shapes for me and poured me a strong cup of tea from the teapot on the cinders, sweetened with sugar. 'Sit up there on the table, Gearóid,' he said and watched me sip the tea down to the last drop.

At home on Christmas night, like every other night, we knelt on the floor, rested our arms on a chair and said the rosary. Mam gave out each decade, as my father and grandparents were too quiet to do it, although my grandfather could be a rogue at times. He was a great man for starting a quarrel just for the fun of it. If he joined two people chatting by the fire, he'd say something to put the wind up one of them. Then, when the other man became hot and bothered and joined in the squabble, Ceaist would quietly walk out of the room and leave them at it.

Even though Mam was religious, she rarely got to Mass on the mainland, as the women on the island went to Mass only now and again, when the weather was calm, while the men went more often. Every Sunday morning, my grandfather Maras Mhuiris recited the rosary in his house for anyone who could not get to the mainland for Mass due to old age, illness or the weather.

When the weather was any way fair, I spent most of my time out and about. Usually I played on my own, but sometimes children from the mainland came to the island to visit their relatives. Whenever I was in the company of other children, I always took charge. I had to be the leader, as I was always used to doing what I wanted. The first child I ever met was Seánín a Phoirt, who was a year older than me and used to visit his grandfather on the island. On the day he came I was not in the mood for playing, so we just rambled around from house to house. Another visitor was Páidín Kearney, a cousin of mine. He was about my age and came from Dunquin with his father, Seán Pheats Tom Kearney, who was a native of the Great Blasket and still kept sheep on the island. They brought along their black and white dog, as he was trained to round up sheep. The family had moved to the mainland on the advice of Páidín's grandparents, who said the island was not a fit place to raise a family, as too many people had left. Seán Pheats Tom seemed pleased with the move to Dunquin, as I often heard him tell my father that it was a lovely place and that the people there were friendly.

He and my father went off to the hill to check the sheep. They were great pals and had both married on the same day in Ballyferriter. Seán Pheats Tom's wife was from the island too, just like Mam. Years later, I heard Seán Pheats Tom say, 'If we didn't marry them, who would we marry? We'd be like two old bachelors on the island. We were highly regarded on the island because we were newly married.'

First I showed Páidín my wooden boats and we sailed them in a pool of water near our house. Then we chased each other around a field until we fell down exhausted. I took him to Cuas a Ghearradh, which was a dangerous pathway between our house and An Tráigh Bháin, with a sheer drop down a cliff into a cave. Mam always warned me to stay away from it, but that only tempted me there all the more. I wanted to show off to Páidín that I could push out a boat to sea and then hop on it myself while it was still moving, so I took him down to the pier where the Micilí were landing after a day's fishing. I begged them to let me show off my strength to Páidín but my plan backfired, as I slipped, hit my head off the seat of the boat and had to run home to Mam with a bloody nose. I didn't see Páidín again until I made my very first trip to the mainland. I was four years of age.

Out of the blue, Mam announced that I would be going to Mass in Dunquin the following Sunday.

Muiris Ua Caomhánaigh, who was called Kruger. He was a well-known shopkeeper, publican and guest house owner in Dunquin. Courtesy of the National Library of Ireland, Colman Doyle Collection.

I couldn't wait, as it meant I could go into Kruger's shop and pick out my own sweets. I was addicted to sweets and ate as many of them as I could lay my hands on, with no limits, as there was never any mention that too many of them were bad for me. I was excited about seeing Kruger too, as I had heard so many yarns about him and knew he was popular with all the islanders. To me, he sounded like a character from my comics, as there was always some drama or other about him. Once Faeilí had come home from Kruger's with a pound of candle grease instead of a pound of lard. When he fried his mackerel, the house looked as if it had caught fire with the amount of smoke pouring out of it. But lard or no lard, he still ate the fish and made sure to tell Kruger about the candle grease on his next visit to Dunquin.

On the morning of my trip, Mam polished my black laced shoes and took out a new pair of white ankle socks for me. She dressed me up in a navy and white sailor suit that had come by post from America. I walked down to the quay in between my father and Faeilí, who were decked out in navy suits, white shirts, ties, dark pullovers, black shoes and peaked caps. The sea looked like a sheet of glass, as it was calm, which meant our clothes would not be destroyed by the sea spray.

We landed at Faill Mór in Dunquin and climbed up the steep, twisted pathway from the pier. Then we strolled to Saint Gobnait's Church in Ballintemple for 11 a.m. Mass. A crowd of people were gathered outside. Dad and I squeezed in among them and stood by the wall to listen to Mass, while Faeilí went inside.

The Child

After Mass, my cousin Páidín Kearney and his father, Seán Pheats Tom, came over to us. Soon more local children gathered around us, among them Breandán, Seán and Pat Ferriter. All eyes were glued on me, as I was the stranger and dressed very differently to all the other boys. They looked me up and down from head to toe and seemed fascinated by me. But I took no notice and mixed easily with them, as I was not at all shy.

The gang of us headed off towards Kruger's shop. I couldn't wait to get there. Even the name of the shop fascinated me, although Kruger was not the real name of its owner, Muiris Ua Caomhánaigh. It so happened that when Muiris was a schoolboy, the schoolmaster picked two teams to play a game of ball, with Muiris and his classmate Seán Walsh as captains. He gave Seán the name 'Kaiser' and called Muiris 'Kruger'. The name stuck. Muiris spent many years in America and used to boast that during his time there he had been Al Capone's right-hand man, acted as an advance agent for the great Victor Herbert and was a bodyguard for de Valera. When he returned and set up his business in the heart of Dunquin, he decided to call it Kruger's.

Most of the islanders shopped at Kruger's. They also bought from Hannah Daly at the post office and Kate Foley, who ran a shop at the top of the harbour. But Kruger's was the most popular, maybe because it was roomier for people to hang around and chat.

When we landed at Kruger's, my heart pounded with excitement. I looked up in wonder at the big sign over the door, showing its name. I couldn't believe I was there. We walked through the open wooden door. The counter was on our right, stacked with newspapers, old and new, among them *The Kerryman* and the Sunday papers. And there was Kruger himself standing behind the counter, a massive, broad-shouldered, tall man with a huge head, wearing a cap. He was just as I had expected him to be, a tough, burly character, larger than life. 'And who is this fine lad?' he asked in a loud, gruff voice, looking down at me. 'Don't tell me it's the loneliest boy in the world! Gearóid, you're very welcome to Kruger's,' he said, reaching out to shake my hand. I noticed his small finger was crooked and that it stood apart from the rest.

I was just about to panic, as I couldn't see the sweets. Then Kruger ducked under the counter and brought up cans of hard-boiled sweets and mouth-watering Cleeve's toffees, which came in big chunks and had to be cut and weighed. 'Take your pick,' he said to me. 'It's on the house.' I asked for a mixture of toffees and bulls-eyes. The men stood chatting while all the children squeezed onto the couch in the shop. Dad treated us to biscuits and a bottle of red lemonade or orange squash, whichever we fancied. He bought a packet of Kimberly and Marietta biscuits to bring home, a bag of chunky Geary's biscuits, two pounds of sugar, a pound of raisins, a plug of Clarke's and Clune's tobacco, ten Player's cigarettes and a pound of butter as a back-up for Mam's homemade butter. Kruger stuffed the lot into Dad's big canvas bag. He bought a Sunday paper too, as Mam and Dad enjoyed reading the news. They had a habit of reading a newspaper together and often spread it out on the kitchen table and commented on each report as they went along. *The Kerryman* was popular on the island and Seán Fillí, the postman, collected two copies on the mainland every Friday or Saturday, depending on the weather.

When we left Kruger's and said goodbye to everyone, I was happy enough to be going back to the island. I liked being on familiar ground and felt I had more freedom there than children had on the mainland, as the children from Dunquin seemed more disciplined and confined than me. Nothing had fazed me about the trip, maybe because I was used to mixing with people. As well as that, apart from the long walk from the quay to the church, I had seen only a tiny part of Dunquin, as it was a short stroll from the church to Kruger's. Nothing would have tempted me to stay on the mainland, except maybe Kruger's shop.

Mam was waiting at the slipway to welcome us back and squeezed me tight when I stepped out of the boat, saying how glad she was that we were home, as she had feared the weather might change for the worse and we might be stranded. She always worried about me when I was away from the house, even if I was only

Islanders amongst visitors, late 1920s. Gearóid's father is
third from the right in front.

rambling around the island, as she considered it to be
a dangerous place. Still, apart from giving me a few
warnings, she never restricted my roaming, so much
so that I got to know all the islanders well and any
strangers who came to the island.

On Sundays during the summer months, day
trippers from nearby Valentia Island came to the
island on a motorboat. They climbed up the slipway,
lugging fiddles, melodeons and baskets of food, and
sat in front of our house in our big field, which was

uncultivated, as the soil was poor. I always plonked myself in the middle of them and they fed me so many tomato sandwiches that I turned against tomatoes for life. The islanders usually joined them for some jigs and reels and always made them feel welcome, as people on the Great Blasket had great time for the people from Valentia and knew many of them well through the Valentia Lifeboat Station. At the time, my grandfather Ceaist was good friends with a family from Valentia named Lavelle.

Seánín Mhicil, our neighbour, always joined in the music sessions, as he was a mighty fiddler. He played in the local, simple style, which was strong on rhythm and left out ornamentation. At home we had a wind-up gramophone and a stack of seventy-eight records by singers such as John McCormack, Delia Murphy and Denis Cox as well as some by fiddle players, among them Michael Coleman, and the Kilfenora and Tulla *céilí* bands. Seánín Mhicil often borrowed the gramophone to pick up new tunes suitable for a Kerry set, which consists of six dance tunes: five jigs and a hornpipe, or six jigs. He practised them for hours night after night by candlelight, alone in a bolted bedroom, until he perfected the tunes. Then he belted them out for the Sunday day trippers as well as many of his older tunes, some of which he picked up from my father and grandfather.

Seánín was a dedicated musician and even made his own fiddles. First he drew an outline of the fiddle on a block of wood. Then he carved out each piece, joined them and inserted the strings, which he bought from the mainland, usually in Dingle. The tradition of making fiddles on the island went back to 1894, when Peaidí Mharas Ó Dálaigh, who was living on Inis Mhicileáin at the time and had a great interest in music, visited the lighthouse at An Tiaracht and met a lightkeeper there who played the fiddle. Peaidí took an outline of his fiddle and made his first violin with driftwood brought in by the sea, although the quality of the wood was poor. That began a tradition of making fiddles on the island, usually in wintertime, when work was slack.

As well as getting to know the day trippers, I also made friends with the holiday-makers, especially those who stayed with Mary Pheats Mhicí. Every summer she kept three holiday-makers. Each guest came at separate times and stayed for a fortnight. I was fascinated by one of them, a stern-looking Scottish man named Ian Moffat Pender, whom we always called Fear an Chóta. Although gentle at heart, in appearance he was a bear of a man with a big curly moustache. He dressed in a kilt, long, thick stockings and brown boots. I had never before seen anyone like him and roared with laughter the first time I saw him. When Faeilí laid eyes on him, he said he was big enough to eat a pig's head. That made him seem even more hilarious to me. I was convinced he had come to the island solely to entertain me and I couldn't get enough of him.

In our house we always rose at the crack of dawn, as my father and grandfather would be heading off to fish or to tend to the sheep, my mother would be busy whipping clothes off the beds for washing or scrubbing the house and my grandmother would make an early start on her knitting or baking. After breakfast I'd run all the way up to the top of the village to the house of Mary Pheats Mhicí. Like my mother, she was a dinger on cleanliness. Her whitewashed home gleamed inside and out, from top to bottom. Mam always said there was a certain refinement about Mary Pheats Mhicí, and indeed about all her family. John Millington Synge called her 'my little hostess' and once described how she had done her best to make him comfortable when he stayed in her father's house in 1905: 'She took off her apron, and fastened it up in the window as a blind, laid another apron on the wet earthen floor for me to stand on, and left me to myself.' She made such an impact on him that she became the prototype for Pegeen Mike in Synge's play *The Playboy of the Western World*.

When I'd arrive at the house of Mary Pheats Mhicí to see Fear an Chóta, she'd appear at the door dressed in a navy, floral, cross-over apron, usually with a broom or a cloth in her hand. 'Come in, Gearóid. He's not up yet,' she'd say, knowing well my reason for calling. I'd go inside, perch myself on a small stool at the side of the hearth facing the door and wait impatiently for Fear an Chóta. Eventually he'd appear, crouched low to come through the doorway, as he was extremely tall. He'd look down at me and say in Irish, 'It's yourself there.' Then he'd settle himself at the kitchen table, which was always laid with a starched white cloth, and tuck into a breakfast of crunchy toast and a runny boiled egg. I'd think of what Faeilí had said about the pig's head and get a fit of giggling. Once finished, he'd grab hold of his big cane, which resembled the sticks used by cattle drovers in Australia, and beckon to me. 'We'll go for a walk so, over the hill.' Hand in hand, we'd stroll towards the west side of the island. Whenever I tired, he'd turn around straight away and take me back to Mary Pheats Mhicí. 'Ye weren't long,' she'd say.

Fear an Chóta spent all his days walking the mountains and all his nights chatting by the fire to Mary Pheats Mhicí's sons, Seán and Muiris. Both young men were well read and at the time owned a copy of every book ever written about the Blasket Islands. They passed on their love of reading to me and years later gave me a copy of *The Islandman*, which is one of the most famous books written by a native of the Blasket Islands. Even when Mary Pheats Mhicí and her family left the island, Fear an Chóta kept up contact with them and often stayed on the mainland with them, and later at Baile an Teampaill with Mary Pheats Mhicí's sister, Kate, who was known as the princess and was the wife of Seán Ó Cathasa.

Another of Mary Pheats Mhicí's annual guests was the teacher and writer Risteard Ó Glaisne, who was a native of Bandon in County Cork, a member of the Methodist community and a supporter of Irish republicanism. Risteard had a limp and, unlike Fear an Chóta, who spent his time strolling, he stayed inside typing or sat outside with Seán and Muiris, chatting about fishing or the economy. I made sure to visit Risteard often but Mary Pheats Mhicí would always warn me, 'Whatever you do, Gearóid, don't disturb Risteard while he's typing.' He entertained me by giving me picture books, mostly of the 1916 Rising, with photos of guns, tanks and famous men like de Valera and Collins.

Another of Mary Pheats Mhicí's yearly guests was Criostóir Mac Cárthaigh, a teacher from Cork. He was the cleanest man I ever saw. Every morning he appeared in Mary Pheats Mhicí's kitchen all spruced up, spotless in a crisp white shirt unbuttoned at the neck with his sleeves rolled up and a pair of open-toe sandals and stockings on his feet. His sandals enthralled me, as the men of the island wore only shoes or hobnailed boots. When they took off their boots by the fire at night, they usually had a hole in their stockings and their big toes stuck out. I used to marvel at Criostóir's big toes twiddling around inside his stockings, as I expected them to pop out any minute. He loved swimming and when I'd tell Mam that I was going up to see Criostóir, she'd hand me my swimming togs to put on inside my trousers. I paddled at the edge while he swam and he always swam diagonally, as he knew the beach was dangerous. One day the weather was so cold that he never got down in the sea, so I threw water at him instead. He chased me all over the strand, shouting my name. I laughed my head off. He loved taking photos too, especially of Beginis, Inis Tuaisceart and the mountains. When my father spoke of Criostóir, he used to say, 'He's dry. Not a drop to be had.' By that he meant that Criostóir was a teetotaller and brought no drink to the island, perhaps unlike Mary Pheats Mhicí's other two guests, who may have brought alcohol with them to share.

Outside her house, by a creek of turf, Mary Pheats Mhicí kept a *birdeog*, which is a shallow wicker basket used for carrying turf to the fire. If Mary Pheats Mhicí was in a good mood, which she normally was, I'd sit in the *birdeog* with two sticks in my hand and pretend I was in a *naomhóg*, rowing away on the high seas. One day when I called she was in a fluster and banned me on the spot from playing in the wicker basket. Her son Muiris was dashing around the place with a bucket of whitewash, painting everything in sight, even the outhouses. Mary Pheats Mhicí had taken down all the ware from the dresser and started washing the lot in a pan of hot water. I didn't stay long. When I called back a few days later the place was shimmering, with all the whitewashing done and fresh sand strewn on the kitchen floor to protect it. A crisp new white cloth draped the table. I got the fright of my life when I saw that the table was laid with glass bowls of little balls of butter, glass bowls of small sugar

This picture was taken after the stations on the Great Blasket in the early 1950s outside the old schoolhouse. Back row (*l–r*): Tom Pheaidí Mharas Ó Dálaigh, Faeilí, Gearóid and Seán Sheáisí; middle row (*l–r*): Maras Mhaidhc Léan Ó Guithín, Seánín Mhicil and unknown; front row (*l–r*): Gearóid's father Seán Cheaist Ó Catháin, Peaidí Beag Ó Dálaigh, Seán Fillí, Seán Mhaidhc Léan Ó Guithín and Peaidí Mharas Ó Dálaigh.

cubes and tiny spoons, which I was unaware were egg spoons. As everything was so small, I got it into my head that leprechauns must be coming for tea. I ran home straight away, not wanting to meet them, as I was afraid of them. When I told Mam my story, she explained to me that Mary Pheats Mhicí was getting ready for the arrival of Father Tom Moriarty, the parish priest from Ballyferriter, and assured me that leprechauns would not be coming for tea.

The islanders loved Father Tom, as he was down to earth and fitted in well with them. They knew his brother Jonathan too, as he was the local wool merchant and owned a pub and a shop in Dingle. On the night of Father Tom's arrival, Mary Pheats Mhicí let me sleep in her house. When Father Tom got up the next morning, I was there, perched on my stool, waiting for him to make his entrance. I was half afraid of him, as he was old and I feared certain old men. I don't know why.

On 15 August every year Father Tom heard confessions, sitting outside on a chair, and celebrated Mass in the old schoolhouse on the island to mark the feast day of the Assumption, which we called Lá le Muire sa bhFomhair, which means Our Lady's Day in Autumn. It also happened to be my mother's birthday and she took pride in that, because she had great devotion to Our Lady. It was a huge day for the islanders and everyone dressed in their Sunday best. Sometimes Father Tadhg Ó Murchú, a teacher from Saint Finbarr's College in Cork, said the annual Mass. He had been visiting the island since the 1930s and was known as An Sagairtín Deas. One year he presented the islanders with a beautiful statue of Our Lady. From then on, Mam, her mother, Mary Pheats Mhicí and June Mháire Eoghain strolled to the school

Tom Pheaidí Mharas O Dálaigh was a great boat maker, carpenter and fiddler.

every day to say a rosary at the statue. Mam often took me along, although I much preferred roaming the island from house to house.

I often called to Tom Pheaidí Mharas Ó Dálaigh, a great fiddler, carpenter and boat maker who lived behind us. I'd stand at the door of his outhouse, which had once been a dwelling house, and watch him carve a *súgán* chair or make or mend a *naomhóg*, which was more curved than a Connemara currach, although the same wood was used for both. Tom's family and the Micilí on the island had supplied the islanders with boats for years, going back to the days of my grandfathers' youth. They were master craftsmen and built two types of boats: a three-oar *naomhóg* and a four-oar, which was a bigger, heavier version and used for work such as fishing or transporting sheep. A typical *naomhóg* had four seats and was twenty-six feet long and over four feet wide, with the prow and the stern rising high above the water and the stern narrowing considerably. The boat's frame had an intricate, lattice-type interlacing, which was fitted with a canvas covering.

Sometimes I swept up the wood shavings on the floor for Tom. When he sprinkled the splinters on the fire my eyes nearly popped out of my head watching the flames take off, as fire fascinated me. Even if my grandfather Ceaist was only lighting the hearth, I'd stand at his shoulder and watch with anticipation as he stacked the back with small sods of turf, their heather already burned off, topped them with kindling and bits of paper and then set them alight with a few drops of paraffin oil.

If Tom was in a leisurely mood, he whittled by the fire until the wood took a shape he fancied. Whittling was a popular pastime with the islanders, among them my grandfather Ceaist. One day Tom said, 'Gearóid, look at the trawler in An Tráigh Bháin. What kind of a shape is she? What colour is she? Is her mast covered with a sail today?' By the time I'd have answered all his questions, he'd have carved an exact model of the trawler for me.

Tom loved a bit of fun and was a great storyteller. One day he told me that the outhouse he worked in had once been the home of Tom Kearney, who had emigrated to America. But, he added, after dying in America, Tom Kearney came back to his home in the Great Blasket and was now fast asleep at the other end of the outhouse in the remains of an old bed. He said to me, 'Gearóid, I need a bit of wood that's below near Tom's bed. You'll have to sneak down there, be as quiet as a mouse and get the wood for me. But whatever you do, don't wake Tom Kearney.'

If I happened to call to Tom's house at dinnertime he'd always invite me in for a bite to eat. On one such day he had a pig's head and turnip cooking in an iron pot on the embers and potatoes boiling in another pot on a crane hanging over the fire. He sat me down at the table, took out the pig's head, cut off its ears, minced a little meat with a knife, mashed in some potato and turnip and put it in front of me, saying, 'Now Gearóid, take your time and watch in case you choke yourself. Swallow it slowly and straight down then once it has passed Fochais Bhéal A' Bhealaigh,' which is a submerged rock near Beginis.

One night I overheard my grandfather Ceaist telling my father that it was time they were heading off for the house of Séamus Mhéiní, as Tom and the rest of the island men were having a get-together there to celebrate having sold their sheep and wool. I kicked up a stink as I wanted to go too. Eventually my grandfather gave in and said he would take me, but only if I brought along my crock, which was a pound-size jam jar, as everyone would be bringing their own container for stout.

The music got underway without delay, with four fiddlers among the gathering: my father, my grandfather Ceaist, Seánín Mhicil and Tom. I was enjoying myself to no end, plonked in the middle of the men, when Tom came over to me and said, 'Gearóid, you have no drink.' He poured some stout from a barrel into my jar, which I drank on the spot. I got sick out of my mind. As I left with my grandfather, Tom tapped his fingers on a barrel of Guinness, shook his head and said, 'Ceaist, he's not ready for it yet.'

When my mother saw the state of me, she gave my grandfather a fine scolding. He made no excuses, sat down by the fire and lit his pipe.

I always took great delight in watching my grandfather light up his pipe. It was like a ritual. First he took out his penknife, as all the men on the island carried a penknife to clean their pipes, apart from Seán Sheáisí, who never smoked. Then he scooped out the remains of the old tobacco and hopped the pipe off the palm of his hand to empty out the debris, which he put into the pipe's silver cover. The cover came in handy, especially if he was smoking outdoors on a windy day. Then he took a square of Clune's tobacco, which was as solid as a sod of turf, peeled off enough to fill his pipe and squashed the tobacco in his hand to make it flaky. He packed the tobacco into his pipe, topped it up with the debris from the cover and set it alight with an ember from the fire, which he scooped out with the pipe's cover. Then he settled back in his chair and puffed away to his heart's delight, pleasure written all over his face. A beautiful, strong aroma filled the kitchen, as Clune's tobacco had a much heavier scent than Clark's tobacco, which my father smoked.

I got it into my head that I should have a pipe myself. As my grandfather seemed to enjoy his pipe so much, I convinced myself that tobacco must have a sweet taste. My father made a pipe for me from seaweed root. It looked just like a clay pipe. I used to fill it with turf and smoke it. Sometimes I stuffed it with paper instead. One day I found tobacco debris on the table from my father's pipe. I packed it into my own pipe, smoked it and almost choked on the spot.

One man on the island decided it was time to curb my wayward ways and put an end to my rambling. His name was Seán Tom Kearney. Whenever I dropped in to Seán Tom at dinnertime his kitchen would be filled with vapour rising from a pot of bacon and dark yellow turnip and another pot with potatoes. He always fed me a generous plateful, and once I had satisfied my hunger I'd hop up to go home. One day, being the rascal that he was, he stopped me in my tracks and told me to sit down again. He landed a big leather-

Gearóid's paternal grandmother, June Eoghain Bháin, and his father standing outside their house on the Great Blasket.

bound book on the table, banged it with his cane and said, 'We must put you to school.' I ran home to my mother, screaming. Being wild and free, any mention of confinement frightened the daylights out of me. I cried all day long and never again darkened his door. Any time Mam and I bumped into him on our way to visit her parents, I'd hide under her coat and hear him moan, 'You haven't gone to school yet.'

Mam was concerned about my schooling too and she taught me how to recognise words by linking them with pictures, as most of my books were pictorial.

When she read to me, she moved her finger slowly from one word to the next. Every now and then she pointed to the picture by the text to explain certain words. She taught me how to count numbers on my abacus, which was a board with small, moveable, coloured balls on rows of string. When it came to teaching me how to write numbers, she had her own special way. To draw the number eight, she said to me, 'Gearóid, just draw two seagull eggs, one on top of the other.' I had trouble with the number four, as I always seemed to write it backwards, maybe because I was left-handed.

As I was practising writing numbers at the kitchen table at home one morning, my grandmother called me over to the hearth. She put her knitting down on her lap, took my hand and said she wanted to say goodbye to me, as she was going into hospital later that day. Then she kissed me gently on the forehead. When she walked down the stony path to the slipway, with my father and my grandfather supporting her at either side, Mam and I followed to wave goodbye as she set off on her journey across the sea.

Weeks later, she still hadn't come home. I pestered Mam every day to tell me what was keeping her. Eventually, with sadness in her eyes, she told me the truth. My grandmother had died in hospital some weeks before and had been buried in Ventry cemetery.

The house seemed empty then, as my grandmother had been a constant, comforting presence and had always played along with me whenever I went into my world of make-believe.

Mam had always been kind to my grandparents, but after my grandmother passed away, she became even more attentive to my grandfather. If his clothes got wet in the rain or at sea, she made sure he changed out of them straight away and she always had dry socks ready and waiting for him when he took off his boots at night.

Once my grandfather and Tiúit knew that I had been told about my grandmother's passing, they spoke openly about her by the fire at night. My grandfather talked about their time in Dingle. 'When I'd go upstairs to the flat after playing the fiddle in Tobac's pub, June would smile and say, "You played well tonight Ceaist, top class," as she would have heard the music below, rising through the ceiling.' Then, he bowed his head and wiped away a tear.

Despite our sorrow, life went on, as there was always much work to be done, both on and off the island.

2

An Island at Work

WEATHER ALWAYS PLAYED a big part on the island. It set the time for sowing seeds, cutting hay, fishing and moving goods and animals to and from other islands or the mainland.

In winter, the landscape on the Great Blasket was dark, dreary, depressing and shrouded in mist, with no growth of any kind – the sea salt made sure of that. The islanders constantly battled for survival against the elements, as ferocious seas battered the island and spurted waves thirty feet high into the air, while vicious winds hammered incessantly. The force of the wind on the island was indescribable. It blasted in from the northeast with a vengeance and rattled our doors and windows, threatening to blow off the rooftops and destroy everything in sight. If my father had to go out in windy conditions, my grandfather would open the door with him, just barely enough to let him out, and lock it again immediately. One night both of them had to go to the outhouse to tie down a cock of hay. They put on their yellow oilskin coats that they usually wore to keep the salt water from their clothes while drawing in lobsters, turned their peaked caps backwards and twined themselves together at the waist to stop one of them from falling.

In westerly or southerly winds the sea spray spewed down the road like a sheet of snow while gigantic waves battered An Tráigh Bháin all the way to the slipway and beyond and changed the sea into a tidal wave of white foam. During such weather the community always felt vulnerable and isolated, completely bound, with no escape.

After violent winds, wreckage usually landed on a nearby pebble beach, known as Tráigh Ghearraí, as the westerly or southerly winds blew directly towards it. My grandfather Ceaist and my father collected wreckage there of timber, containers of paraffin oil, chests of tea and tins of biscuits.

During fog, a deadly silence fell on the island. Nothing would be heard except deafening blasts from the foghorn of An Tiaracht, warning the mariners of the dangers of the sea and giving them a sense of direction.

Sunny summer days were glorious, never too hot or too cold, with the waves sparkling at An Tráigh Bháin and thousands of birds chirping in a deafening crescendo, among them puffins, guillemots, kittiwakes, sea ravens, razorbills, herring gulls and black-backed gulls.

In spring the islanders prepared the fields above An Tráigh Bháin for the setting of potatoes. They turned over every single sod of earth with a spade, then fertilized the earth with cow and donkey manure. They dug holes in the ground along a straight line and dropped in potato slices with sprouting eyes, then they spread seaweed on top and later earth. Once stalks began to show, they earthed the ground again. They also set turnips, cabbage, onions, carrots, parsnips and beetroot there, as the land was good, although it was sandy and needed a lot of fertilizer.

They also sowed hayseed and oats in the spring by scattering them by hand from a bucket. They spent much time debating if the oats should be planted in the same field as the year before or if they should be set where the hay had been, as changing crops from one field to another often improved the yield.

Once April came the islanders' thoughts turned to cutting the turf at An Cró, although it was often early or mid-May by the time they got round to it, as dry weather was needed. First they burned off the *stuaicín*, which is the top side of a bog, made up of sprig, heather, gorse and furze. Some days later they headed off for An Cró again, armed with a turf spade, known as a *sleán*. The shovel had an extra piece jutting out at the side, which stopped the spade from sinking fully into the ground and made it easier to scoop out the turf. And that was important, as cutting turf is a backbreaking job.

When the turf was cut from the bog, the men turned it upside down to dry. They stood each sod of turf on a slant, one against the other, then placed one sod on the flat across the top of the stook. Sometimes it took a week to cut and stook the turf, depending on the weather. Then the drawing home of the turf began. That work was considered easy and was usually done by the women. It was a job I loved. I would set off with Mam and our donkey with a pannier at either side. Every family on the island owned a donkey but there wasn't a single horse to be seen, as horses were too big for the island's terrain. Mam and I would fill each pannier to the brim, then stroll home at our ease and pile the turf in an outhouse.

Taking a cow to the hill to graze was another task I enjoyed. Our cow slept in the cow house at night or rested in a fenced-off field. She needed fresh grass and some days Seán Tom Kearney, my grandfather Ceaist and I would walk her up to Tráigh Ghearraí to graze. Our old dog Sheridan would toddle along with us, roving in and out between our legs. Seán Tom and my grandfather would talk all the way, chatting about everything from the weather to the amount of seaweed fertilizer used for setting vegetables. We'd spend the day on the hill with the cow. We never took the risk of leaving her alone, as she might wander. We'd laze on the grass and eat and drink at our leisure. Every now and then I'd hop up and kick a ball around, but most of the day I sat listening to Seán Tom and my grandfather, as I was a good listener, even at a young age. They recalled fishing expeditions, debated if the fishermen would be short-changed by the buyers and talked about the trip to Inis Tuaisceart to shear the sheep or move them or check the growth, as the land there was a mixture of gorse and grass.

Sometimes I went to the well near Faeilí's house with my mother, where the women of the island washed the clothes by scrubbing them with Lifebuoy or carbolic soap in buckets or in a big wooden vessel known as a *beiste*, with a handle at either side. The well was called Tobar an Phoncáin, which means the well of the Yank. It was named after my granduncle Pádraig Mistéal, who had spent a lot of time in America. At the well the women exchanged all the news of the day, such as what was happening with relatives abroad or how many eggs were being laid.

Fish was a vital source of income for the islanders, especially mackerel and lobster. The fishermen hated to see masses of seals gathered on the strand or basking in the sun on the rocky ledges, as they were avid predators of fish.

Until perhaps the middle of the nineteenth century, the islanders used large timber boats for fishing. Known as seine boats, these vessels were heavy and required a big crew, unlike their replacement, the *naomhóg*, which was smaller and lighter. But heaving and hauling a *naomhóg* to go fishing was hard work. Great strength, balance and skill were needed, not only for carrying the extremely heavy boat, but also for turning it over, which was tricky. If the *naomhóg* fell in the process, serious injury could ensue.

Each *naomhóg* was stored upside down with its bow facing the Great Blasket landing in a sheltered area on a path at the side of the slipway, which had a greasy, bumpy surface and was coated in green algae. It was easier to launch a boat in high tide than in low tide, as a high tide covered the algae.

Each boat was tied with coils of rope and slotted onto four wooden blocks, known as *stáitsí*, which were made from white deal and hammered into the ground. As the canvas on the boats was delicate, keeping the boats high off the ground in a sheltered area, away from grassy patches, wind and rain, helped protect them. In days gone by, when the island had a bigger population, keeping the boats stored far away from the edge of the shore would have made it less tempting for youngsters to take to the sea on a whim. Every pair of oars had its own marking to identify the owner.

Usually each *naomhóg* had a crew of four men. The fishermen always wore a brown scapular to protect them in times of peril and hobnailed boots, as they gave a good grip on a slippery surface. They tied a small whiskey bottle of holy water onto the bow end of the boat with a piece of string. In times of strife, they sprinkled the holy water around the sides of the boat

Seán Mhaidhc Léan and others launching a *naomhóg*.

and on the sea. Most of the fisherman never learned to swim, as they felt it would be better to drown quickly rather than put up a fight. Also, the sea was viewed as a place of work, not of leisure, as the waters around the Great Blasket were strong and dangerous.

To launch the boat, first the men untied it, then each of them slipped under the thwarts and carefully hoisted the boat with their shoulders. As a rule the sturdiest of the men stood under the bow, as it was vital that the man in that position held his footing to ensure the boat wouldn't topple over. Once in position, they steadied themselves and said, 'Are we right?' Then they carefully walked to the edge of the shore, where they tried to avoid being splashed by the waves and getting a soaking even before they took to the sea. They slowly leaned the *naomhóg* to the right-hand side, tried to get it into a position to keel it over and then straightened it up.

When they landed back at the slipway, they reversed the boat into the landing. The man at the stern got out first while the others rowed in as near as possible to the shore. Then two more jumped out. The three men standing in the water lifted the boat up out of the tide while the man on the bow then hopped out and stacked the oars at the side of the slipway. All four men hauled the *naomhóg* up the slipway in an upward position and carefully leaned it over as the man at the bow put his foot on the gunnel. Then a second man put his foot on the gunnel and pulled the *naomhóg* over. Two men slipped underneath while the other two shouldered the boat. Once all the men had the *naomhóg* firmly resting on their shoulders, they carefully climbed up the slipway, always checking with each other to make sure they were all in step. When they reached the *stáitsí*, two men stepped out and helped the other two mount the *naomhóg*.

The lobster season started in May and ran right through until September, although the first pots were

Men launch a *naomhóg* on the slipway of the Great Blasket as Gearóid looks on. Photo: John Petch.

often set as early as Saint Patrick's Day. In his prime, my grandfather Maras Mhuiris made three lobster catches a day: at 4 a.m., 10 a.m. and 3 p.m. Most of the island's fishermen rowed out in their boats in early morning, around 6 a.m., but my uncle Faeilí and his brothers took to the sea at 4 a.m. to beat the predators, such as eels, as some fish travel at night and steal the bait. Some of the islanders went lobster fishing at An Tiaracht. Others stayed close to the Great Blasket. Peaidí Mharas Ó Dálaigh and his sons fished off Inis Mhicileáin, to the west. Most had twenty pots or more. They filled the pots with bait, usually a mixture of fish, including crab, and placed stones at the bottom to sink the pots. They joined the pots together with rope and attached corks and metal buoys to prevent them from drifting. To keep the pots in place, they needed good, calm weather. More often than not they hauled the pots four times daily: twice before dinner and twice after dinner. They packed the lobsters into canvas sacks and stored them near the harbour in big storage pots made from osier twig from the mainland. They often used long stalks of island heather to make the base of the pots. On a good day they might catch between two and three dozen lobsters. Sometimes they fished from dawn until dusk.

I remember going lobster fishing with my father, Faeilí and Maurice Ó Guithín. Faeilí always acted as the haulier, as he had great balance. My heart was in my mouth as I watched him because I was afraid he might topple overboard. He stood with one foot in the middle of the *naomhóg* and the other on the gunwale, with the boat bobbing up and down on the swirling waves. Then he raised the lobster pots with a gaffe, which is a stick with a metal hook, by catching the rope by the cork. He drew in the lobster pots and emptied the lobsters into canvas sacks before filling the pots again with bait and throwing them back into the sea. Then he moved on to the next set of pots. If the catch was poor, he dragged the pots up another hundred yards and set them in a different spot. My father was always praising Faeilí's skill and the durability and

The quay in Dunquin in the mid-1900s.

buoyancy of the *naomhóg*, which he said was the best boat of all for lobster fishing.

On a Friday the fishermen rowed to Dunquin to meet the lobster buyer or they rowed out to Dingle with the catch. If the buyer failed to turn up and the islanders had unloaded their catch at Dunquin and brought it up to the top of the harbour, they would then have to take it to Dingle on a horse and cart. Patience was essential, as the selling process was frustrating. Many of the buyers were stern, argumentative men. The islanders often sold below cost, as the buyers sometimes quoted unfair prices and were never open to negotiation. Their common saying was 'you can like it or lump it'. The islanders rarely kept any lobster for themselves, as they had no liking for it.

Once the lobster season ended in September, the mackerel season began. A crew usually fished with six nets, which they tied together, with the worn net left at the end of the line.

Tending to sheep kept the men busy too, as the Great Blasket was home to hundreds of sheep and most of the islanders kept a flock. Each family had its own sheep markings, in one or more colours. Ours was red. On the day of sheep shearing in the month of June, one of the men went over the mountain at the east side of the Great Blasket early in the morning to check the position of the sheep. They might be grazing at An Cró, An Cnoc or on Ceann Dúbh, which was the furthest point of the island from the village.

Once the islanders found out where the sheep were located, all the active men headed off, my grandfather Ceaist among them, but not Tiúit or my grandfather Maras Mhuiris, who had been a great hunter and walker in his day. Each man carried a canvas bag containing shears, string for tying the sheep, blocks of colour for marking them, buttered bread, strips of bacon and tea in flasks or in a corked whiskey bottle.

All the dogs of the village went too, although none of them were sheep dogs and they weren't trained for rounding up sheep. Most of them were mongrels of every shape, size and colour. Our own big dog scampered along with them. My grandfather Ceaist

Mary Faight (*left*) watches her father (*right*) and another
islander shearing sheep on Tráigh Ghearraí.

had bought him from tinkers in Dingle and named
him Sheridan, which was a slang word he used for
itinerants.

I only walked as far as the derelict outhouses in
the village, which the sheep would be driven to for
shearing, as the three-mile trek to where they were
grazing was too far for a child of my age. I waited with
my grandfather, Maras Mhuiris, outside the main
outhouse for sheep shearing, which was nicknamed
Gerry's house. From there, we had a full view of the
round-up.

I remember standing there on one such day, watching one crowd of men and their dogs heading to the west side and another to the east. The round-up started off peacefully, with the men in a jovial mood. They rounded up their first flock of sheep easily enough and herded them on towards the pen, with the dogs trailing excitedly behind. But just as the sheep were on the point of going into the pen, all hell broke loose and the dogs and sheep scattered in every direction. The men cursed and swore, blamed one another for the breakaway and called their dogs every name under the sun. They flung their caps in the air with temper, yelled angrily at each other and frantically waved their canvas bags, trying to block the sheep and herd them in a different direction. The poor sheep must have been frightened to death, as they are docile creatures by nature. My grandfather Maras Mhuiris shook his stick in the air with rage and stamped his foot. 'Well blasht it! What did I tell them? Didn't I say we should have brought Seán Pheats Tom Kearney over from Dunquin? Isn't he the only man with trained dogs and doesn't he know the island well, being a native himself and his sheep up there among ours? But they wouldn't listen because Faeilí and the rest of them think they know it all. Well now we'll see what they're made of!' Tempers were hot on the hill and the men were on the verge of throwing in the towel and heading back home, but then they gave it another go.

Seán Pheats Tom Kearney (*left*) and Gearóid's father (*right*) in their *naomhóg* on the slipway of the Great Blasket, probably taken in the 1960s.

Eventually they succeeded in their task and rounded up about twenty sheep in a lot. 'They're coming now,' my grandfather shouted to me, pointing his stick in their direction with an air of relief in his voice. Then he picked a good spot for us to watch their approach without causing an obstruction.

Once the sheep were safely inside the outhouse, the men closed any openings with old doors and timber posts from the wrecks. After shearing the sheep, they tied some of them together with strings and drove them back to the mountain and kept others in the outhouses for transfer to Beginis, which was used as a halting ground. The grass on Beginis was thought to be the best in the islands due to its rich saline content, and the sheep would graze there until they were sold or returned again to the Great Blasket. Old sheep past the age of breeding were usually sold off, as were castrated young rams, known as wethers, as culling and husbandry was part and parcel of sheep rearing. The men piled the thick, sheared wool outside the outhouses on the grass and packed it into canvas sacks, which they tied with string and marked with sheep markings to distinguish one herd from another. Then they stored the sacks in the outhouses until a hired trawler came to collect them, along with the sheep for sale.

The sellers sailed on the trawler to Dingle and unloaded the sheep and wool on the quay, where the sale took place. The wool was sold to Father Tom's brother, Jonathan Moriarty, who was the only local wool merchant. A few Dingle butchers, such as the Curran and Moriarty families, would have made a prior agreement with the islanders about buying the sheep and would arrive to collect them. Their prices were tight even though the Blasket sheep were always in great demand, as the Blasket grazing of furze and heather gave sheep a lean texture.

Later in the day, the sellers visited the butchers and got paid on the spot. Being honest and reliable, the islanders then made their way to the Dingle shopkeepers and paid off their debts. If they sold in late autumn they paid off their debts first and used any leftover money for the Christmas fare. If the shopkeepers sensed that the islanders had little or no money for Christmas shopping, they gave them extra time to pay off a debt. The Dingle shopkeepers were kind-hearted, so much so that they probably ended up being out of pocket themselves sometimes.

When it came to money matters especially, the women of the island called all the shots and made sure that everything was above board. They had full control of their men and made sure that after paying off all debts and buying the Christmas fare, any leftover money was spent on needs for the following year, such as clothes or household goods.

My grandfather Ceaist kept sheep over on Inis Tuaisceart, as he had grazing rights there for which he paid a nominal fee to John Moore, an auctioneer in Dingle. The timing of the trip to Inis Tuaisceart was vital. Good weather was essential, as a vast, un-sheltered, ten-mile area lay between the Great Blasket and Inis Tuaisceart and the island had no landing area, unlike An Tiaracht. If the weather took a turn for the worse while the fishermen were rowing in the open area, they would have no hope of survival. And they couldn't stay overnight on the island, as it had no landing spot for a *naomhóg*.

My grandfather Ceaist had the last say on when to go to Inis Tuaisceart, as he was considered a great reader of the weather. Making the decision to go there began well in advance of the trip.

I remember rising with my grandfather at the crack of dawn in summertime, usually in July or August, and walking uphill past An Tráigh Bháin to the fields at the foot of the mountain. From there, he got a clear view of An Tiaracht, Inis Tuaisceart and Ceann Sibéal, which he needed to check a route west-north-west and forecast the weather. At night he checked the moon, as a hazy ring around the moon meant bad weather. The direction of the wind was a vital factor for the trip due to the lack of shelter. The kindest wind of all was a westerly wind. The islanders depended on my grandfather to make the right decision. It was important that they were united in their trust, as to achieve anything at sea they had to agree with each other. Disagreement never helped.

Once my grandfather was satisfied that the time was right to go to Inis Tuaisceart, he'd say to my father, 'Things are looking good, Seán. We'll go tomorrow.' Usually three men went on the trip, along with a few dogs and Tiúit, who was a great boatman. He knew every sandbank and submerged rock in the area and stayed at sea in the boat all day to mind it. Knowing

Filling a *naomhóg* with hay as bedding for a cow to be
taken from the Great Blasket to Dunquin.

they would not be hitting the Great Blasket again
until dusk, the men took plenty of food, including
pig's feet, pig's head and fish. I went on one such trip
but the day was too long for me, as the men worked
until late evening. I had to stay in the boat with Tiúit
all day and fell fast asleep in the bow.

If the men were bringing sheep over and back from
An Tuaisceart, they took two boats. They rounded up
sheep to be moved from Inis Tuaisceart by *naomhóg*,
tied them together with string and led them down to

a big flagstone. There, the men tied the sheep's legs together to stop them budging on the boat, as any movement could cause it to topple over. For balance, they divided the sheep equally among the two boats and carefully laid them on their backs in the bottom of the boats, making sure that they had enough breathing space. They also tied the dogs to the seat of the boat even though, on the whole, dogs were stable travellers. Every man and every animal was cramped for the long journey back to the Great Blasket, but at least the boat was steady, as anything loose in a boat was a danger. All the way home, the men constantly checked the sheep to make sure they had enough air.

Once the summer ended, the islanders cured the fish by salting and layering them in sealed barrels. Then they began preparing for the next fishing season. They checked and mended their fishing nets. To strengthen them, they dipped the nets into a *beiste* – which was the same type of wooden tub the women washed clothes in – full of a hot, brownish liquid dye called *coirt*. Then they hung the nets on a ditch or on a roof to dry. They also checked the strength of their ropes and lobster pots. They mended their lobster pots and made new ones from osier twig. In winter they checked their houses for leaks. They spread canvas rags over the felted roofs and tarred them, having boiled the tar in a big barrel.

At that time of year, I remember my father and grandfather Ceaist sitting in the kitchen with buckets of potatoes at their feet. They carefully examined the potatoes to check if the eyes were sprouting, turning each potato over and over again to make sure. Then they sliced off the sprouting eyes and laid them aside in wooden boxes for replanting. If Faeilí or Tiúit happened to call, they were drawn into the debate about the sprouting eyes.

During the winter many of the men on the island slept a lot by day, especially between the hours of two and five o'clock. Some went to bed while others slept on a chair, a table or a settle, which was a wooden sofa with a curtain in front, behind which various items, such as shoes, were stored or hidden away to give a tidier appearance. Some even visited neighbours' houses for the sole reason of having a snooze there. When Mam and I called in to her parents' house, we often tiptoed around as all the men would be sound asleep, with Faeilí stretched across the table with his head on a cushion, his brother Maraisín Mhuiris asleep on the settle and his father Maras Mhuiris snoring on a chair.

By the time spring came round again, the islanders were well rested and eager to start yet another cycle of work. But in spite of all their hard work, times were tough and getting harder.

3

A Time of Change

ON 22 APRIL 1947, only three months before I was born, the islanders sent a telegram to the Taoiseach, Éamon de Valera, pleading for help: 'Storm bound, distress, send food, nothing to eat.' A few days later, a boat sailed to the island with basic food supplies and a couple of bottles of whiskey.

On Monday, 14 July 1947, Éamon de Valera visited the Great Blasket as part of his personal tour of Ireland's island communities. He sailed to the island on the LE *Macha*. Some viewed the trip as an attempt to renew contact with the rural way of life that inspired his vision of Ireland, as the state of the economy was poor and a general election loomed. De Valera had been to the Great Blasket before, in seek of refuge at the end of the civil war.

At a meeting with his officials back in Dublin, de Valera voiced his concern about the decline of the

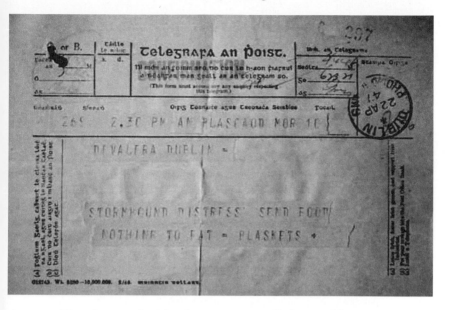

The telegram the islanders were compelled to send because
of an extended period of bad weather in 1947.

island's living conditions. He made it clear that he was
against moving the islanders to the mainland.

In late August, an official from the Department of
Lands and another from the Department of Education
visited the Great Blasket to assess the situation. They
concluded that lack of communication with the outside world was the real problem, not poverty, and they
were convinced that the islanders were keen to leave.

On 15 September 1947, the islanders wrote a letter
to de Valera asking to be told what he intended to

do for them and stating that if he failed to help, the old people on the island would have to move to the mainland to live with friends while the rest would have to emigrate.

In February 1948, de Valera's government fell from power and a coalition government was elected. In early 1950, a further inspection of the Great Blasket took place when two officials from the Land Commission visited the island. In June 1951, de Valera and his party were re-elected to government.

By the early 1950s, the state of life on the Great Blasket had deteriorated greatly, mainly due to old age and infirmity. The number of men going fishing had declined noticeably. As a result, supplies of fish for the islanders fell as well as the amount of fish for sale, which meant less income and more hardship for the fishermen and their families. The days of fishing were well and truly over for most of the islanders and they would be lucky to have two men on board a *noamhóg* when heading out to sea when four men were needed to row. he same was true of sheep rearing and growing crops.

All the islands around Ireland were isolated, but the Great Blasket was extremely remote, especially as it had no reliable means of communication in an emergency, such as an accident, illness or prolonged stormy weather, during which food might become scarce or medical help might be needed. An example of a terrible tragedy on the island happened in January

(*L–r*): Seán Sheáisí, Maras Mhaidhc Léan, Tiúit, Peaidí Mhicil and Pádraig Mistéal. Photo: John Petch.

1947, when the island was cut off by storm and a young islander named Seánín Tom Kearney, who had contracted meningitis, urgently needed medical help. Sadly, the young man suffered much pain and died without any aid.

The post office on the island had a radio telephone that was linked to the Dunquin post office since 1947, but most of the time the island's telephone was broken. It was wind powered and its wind charger flew above the chimney of the post office. Severe wind alone often put it out of order. If the phone was broken when the island was cut off from the mainland and urgent help was needed, the islanders lit a fire at An Gob, which is a headland on the island facing Dunquin. Once people on the mainland spotted the fire, they called the emergency services, usually the Valentia Lifeboat. As those on the mainland would have been unaware of the circumstances of the emergency, the lifeboat came well supplied for most emergencies and with medical personnel on board.

One Sunday evening in late summer 1952, Faeilí, Maraisín Mhuiris, Maras Mhaidhc Léan and Seánín Mhicil rowed back to the Great Blasket with news after being to Mass in Dingle. 'Things are picking up in Dunquin,' Faeilí said. 'We noticed a huge improvement in the number of tourists in Dingle and Dunquin.' His brother Maraisín Mhuiris added, 'We saw bus-loads of tourists coming around Slea Head.' For the first time ever, I heard talk of moving to the mainland when Faeilí said, 'I think we'd be better off over there, wouldn't we?'

Also in 1952, Faeilí and his brother Maraisín Mhuiris as well as Seán Mhaidhc Léan Ó Guithín and his brother Maras Mhaidhc Léan signed a memorandum seeking urgent help and asking to be housed on the mainland. It pointed out that there were now only enough able-bodied men on the island to man two boats and stated, 'We are prepared for any migration, anything to leave the island, but we will be satisfied with a house and one acre, or even a house on the mainland.' It concluded, 'If people at this stage of civilisation and standard of living only realised what hardships of mind and body we endure, we are sure that they would raise their voices and rally to our cause.'

In November 1952, more than five years after de Valera's visit, the order was given to evacuate the island and the wheels were set in motion to move the islanders to the mainland.

The younger men, like Faeilí and his brother, seemed to want to go. But the older men, most of whom had spent all their life on the island, were non-committal. A common saying on the island was 'it's God's will'. And that seemed to be their attitude. They took life a day at a time, in whatever shape or form it came in, and never complained. They put up no argument and made no drama about leaving. My grandfather Ceaist made no comment whatsoever. There was a certain calmness about it all.

Somehow, I sensed my mother wanted to go. In recent months she had seemed restless and had begun to spend more and more time on the mainland with her sister Kate, who lived in Beenbawn, outside Dingle, and with her sister Lís, who lived in Graffies, near the village of Feothanach. When she visited them she always took me with her, which meant I was also spending less time on the island.

When she was at home she whiled away a lot of the day with her mother or Mary Pheats Mhicí. She must have found the summer days especially long and lonely, as my father would have been gone from dawn to dusk. She was also becoming more concerned about my schooling, as I was nearly six years of age. Making sure I got an education became her priority.

But I think she'd had enough of island life by then and longed to leave its severity and isolation and live in cosier conditions. Being a young woman, still only in her thirties, she must have craved the company of people her own age.

To begin the evacuation process, in 1953 the Land Commission came up with a plan of moving three farming families from Dunquin and offering their homes and land to three families from the Great Blasket. They gave the Dunquin families the option of moving to bigger farms in counties Kildare and Meath. All of them accepted the offer, among them Ulick Moran, his wife – who happened to be Kruger's sister – and their sons. The family moved to County Kildare in April 1953. The Land Commission offered my parents the Morans' house and land. Without any great debate, they accepted.

Soon my father began moving our belongings to Dunquin, little by little. Our home on the island started to look bare then, especially when he shifted the kitchen dresser. In July, when he was moving some more furniture, he took me over to see our new house. It nestled nicely between two rolling hills in a sheltered area in the townland of Baile na hAbha, on the outskirts of Dunquin on the road to Ballyferriter.

Three other houses stood nearby, with a stream running by all four homes.

Ours was a huge two-storey house with a big wooden front door, two large windows at the front and two windows upstairs at each gable end. In comparison to our home on the Great Blasket, it was a mansion. But I wasn't excited about living there, as I didn't care if we stayed on the island or moved to the mainland.

The house had a gated front garden with a concrete wall and hedge overlooking the main road. It also had two adjoining cow houses, one at either side. One of the cow houses had two concrete steps to ease the task of loading milk churns on and off a cart. My father described the farm as being comfortable enough for five cows. The fields had a slight incline and ran along at both sides of the house.

When my father opened the front door, a steep staircase with bare boards faced us. He warned me to be careful climbing it. A big kitchen was positioned to the right of the stairs, with two adjoining rooms. It was strange to see our dresser in the kitchen, which had a big open fireplace with a crook hanging overhead and two painted cupboards, probably made by my father. Downstairs also had a back kitchen. The upper floor had four bedrooms. The house had no bathroom, running water or electricity.

I was playing on the stairs, humming to myself and hopping from one step down to the next, when a girl walked into the hall. Her name was Máirín Ferriter and she lived next door. She was about my own age and was the sister of Breandán, Seán and Pat, whom I had met on my first trip to the mainland. We strolled around the house and went out to the back garden, which was wild and overgrown. It had lots of fuchsia bushes and apple trees in blossom, swaying in the summer breeze. Its rich growth and sweet scent fascinated me, as I had never seen or smelled so much flora. Máirín and I sat on a step at the back door, facing the stream. Soon I fell sound asleep, as my father and I had made an extra-early start that morning.

During the next few weeks, my father continued to go over and back with our belongings. One morning Mam said to me, 'We must pack all your things today, Gearóid – books, comics, toys, the lot. You can keep back a book and two toys.' I knew then that the time was close for leaving.

4

The Evacuation

ON THE MORNING of 5 September 1953, Mam and I strolled up the pathway to Barr a' Bhaile for the last time to say goodbye to my grandparents and uncles. My grandmother hugged me tight and told me that I would have great fun on the mainland, as I would have plenty of pals my own age there. My uncle Maraisín Mhuiris promised to call to see us any time he was in Dunquin. My grandfather pressed some coins into my hand, patted my head and said, 'Now you'll be able to drop into Kruger's every day.' Faeilí folded his arms, stood back against the wall and laughed, 'And Gearóid, when you see Kruger, tell him your uncle Faeilí was wondering if he has any lumps of candle grease for sale!'

Soon after going home, my parents and I left the house for the last time, along with my grandfather Ceaist, our terrier Shep by his side (Sheridan had died of old age by then). Dad put a padlock on the front door and we all walked down the slipway together, lugging the last of our belongings, among them two lobster pots full of chickens. I carried a hurley in one hand and a small bag in the other, with my teddy bear peeping over the top.

All the islanders had gathered on the quay to wave us off. When we stepped into the *naomhóg*, Dad placed one lobster pot in the bow and the other in the stern. Shep settled himself down beside my grandfather. Faeilí came with us to help, while Seán Fillí, Seán Mhaidhc Léan and Maras Mhaidhc Léan rowed along beside us in another *naomhóg* full of more of our belongings, mostly in canvas bags. We pulled away from the Great Blasket to the sound of the dog barking, the hens clucking, the older islanders crying and the waves crashing all around us, bobbing us up and down on the sea.

We were the first of the islanders to be evacuated. From then on, others began to leave. Dan O'Brien, the Irish Land Commission inspector from Tralee, was responsible for meeting the islanders and collecting the purchase agreement forms, which the islanders had to sign as proof that they were willing to leave their island homes forever and settle on the mainland. John Goulding, another official, was also involved in the evacuation. Under the agreement, the islanders who accepted homes on the mainland became owners of those houses, as well as the land that came with them, subject to the payment of an annuity. They kept their ownership of their homes on the Great Blasket and the right to graze their sheep there. The resettlement of the islanders was the first operation of its kind ever carried out by the Land Commission.

Although the day appointed for the final evacuation of the island was Tuesday, 17 November 1953, the island wasn't fully evacuated until 1954. Many of the islanders had left by Christmas, among them Mary Pheats Mhicí. Her sons Seán Mhaidhc Léan and Maras Mhaidhc Léan, along with my uncle Maraisín Mhuiris, stayed behind, as they had rams on the hill and wanted to take them to the mainland. But the weather broke and they were forced to stay on the island for Christmas. On Christmas Eve they had no candle and no oil, but they found wax slates, which had been washed ashore during the war, and also cotton. They melted the wax and placed it in a vessel and used the cotton to make a wick. It was their only source of light. They left the island on 27 December 1953.

The last people to leave the island were the Micilí: Seán Mhicil Ó Súilleabháin, his wife June Mháire Eoghain and their sons Seánín Mhicil, Peaidí Mhicil and Maidhc Mhicil. Their daughter Lís, a daughter-in-law of the famous writer Tomás Ó Criomhthain, told of her last visit to her family on the island in a letter she wrote to George Chambers: 'It was quite late in the day when we left Dingle Harbour. We were greeted

Arriving at Dingle Pier after being evacuated on the *Saint Laurence O'Toole* (*l–r*): Seán Sheáisí, Pádraig Mistéal, Seánín Mhicil, Seán Fillí, Seán Mhaidhc Léan and Faeilí. Courtesy of the *Irish Examiner*.

by a pitiful sight. We visited the Ó Súilleabháin, now known as the lightkeepers, for they are the last ones left on the rock. We cried and laughed together but we could only stay an hour. We sadly bade them goodbye. It was to be our last time together on the island.' Her family left the island on 14 November 1954. Perhaps the words of her father, Seán Mhicil, reflected the thoughts of many of the islanders, especially the aged: 'I don't want to die here unaided. My wish is to be buried in the graveyard at Fionntrá. I want to be buried with my ancestors, in our own graveyard. When I was young and strong, I never found fault with this place. I thought it as good a place as anywhere else in the world. We had the fishing and people could depend on one another. But alas, that day is gone. Now, there is no-one left. The weather is worsening and the sea is choppy. A boat may not be able to venture out for weeks if I die here. But, when I was young, I preferred this place to anywhere on earth. I am heartbroken leaving it.'

During our time on the Great Blasket, we had lived as a community. Now everyone was scattered on the mainland. Like us, Tiúit moved into one of the evacuated houses in Dunquin, as did Maidhc Faight and his sister Mary, who set up home in a house at Carhue in Dunquin. My grandfather Maras Mhuiris, Seán Mhicil, Mary Pheats Mhicí, Peaidí Mharas Ó Dálaigh and their families all moved into new cottages in Dunquin, built especially for them in an area called Baile na Rátha, although the houses were not near each other. All the islanders who moved to Dunquin were given commonage rights to cut turf at bogs near their holdings, such as at Mount Eagle or Maoilinn. It was an important concession, as turf was the main fuel used at the time.

Seán Sheáisí and his mother Lís moved into a new housing estate in Dingle, called Marian Park,

Seán Team Kearney (*right*) at his daughter's house in
Muiríoch and a visitor.

while Seán Tom Kearney and Peats Shéamais went
to live with their daughters in Muiríoch, north of
Ballyferriter. Seán Fillí went to live with his sister in
Dingle and Muiris Mór moved to Ventry. Before the
evacuation began, Séamus Mhéiní had left the island
to live with his mother Méiní at Baile Uí Cínn, near
Dunquin harbour.

The Great Blasket had lost its people. Its evacuation
marked the end of an eccentric, isolated way of life,
the roots of which had been planted many generations
before.

5

The Past

UNTIL THE GREAT BLASKET was abandoned in 1954, the island had been continuously inhabited for three hundred years. Evidence shows that the Great Blasket was occupied during the Iron Age and early Christian times, while legal documents state that in the thirteenth century a family called the Ferriters leased the island from the Earl of Desmond for an annual rent of two hawks. The Ferriters, a powerful Anglo-Norman family, held much land in west Kerry, including Ballyferriter, which was named in their honour, as was the Great Blasket itself, which was once called Ferriter's Island.

Perhaps the most famous of the Ferriter clan was its chieftain and poet, Pierce, who fought in the Cromwellian wars on the side of the confederates and was executed at Cnocán na gCaorach in Killarney in

Looking at the Great Blasket village from Bun a' Bhaile,
probably taken in the 1930s.

1653 after being defeated at nearby Ross Castle. Much
mention is made of him in Blasket Island folklore,
especially about places where he outwitted the English
or showed great courage. On the northern face of the
Great Blasket stands Pierce's Cave, which Pierce used
as a hiding place when fleeing from the English. His
troubles are remembered in storytelling as well as
in the verse he is said to have composed in the cave.
Ferriter's Castle stood on a small headland known as

Rinn a' Chaisleáin, north of the island's landing place. Later, the islanders used the site as a burial place for unbaptised babies, those who took their own lives and shipwrecked sailors.

After the Desmond rebellion ended in 1583, the Blasket Islands became the property of supporters of the Crown and fell into the hands of two English adventurers named Champion and Stone. Eventually the islands were sold to Sir Richard Boyle, who later became the Earl of Cork.

In September 1588 two ships from the Spanish Armada were wrecked in the Blasket Sound, while two other ships from the fleet, the *San Juan* and the *San Juan Batista*, took shelter there from storms for six days and survived. Evidence from Spanish documents of the time suggests that the Great Blasket was inhabited at the end of the sixteenth century. In 1756 Charles Smith reported that five or six families were living on the island and that all of them were in exceptionally good health in comparison to people on the mainland.

During the nineteenth century the island had an influx of families due to population growth and evictions on the mainland. In the baptismal register of the Blasket Islands for the years 1808 to 1817, eight family names are recorded, six of which appear often during the nineteenth and early twentieth centuries: Ó Cheárna, Ó Guithín, Ó Duinnshléibhe, Ó Séaghdha, or Ó Sé, Ó Criomhthain and Ó Catháin.

A group of cheerful young women. Gearóid's mother is
on the extreme right. Courtesy of the National Folklore
Collection, UCD. Photo: Thomas Waddicor.

In the official census register of 1821 the population
of the Great Blasket is shown as 128. At the time, the
inhabitants of the island occupied eighteen houses.

In the main, the houses were long, dark, one-storey
buildings with a loft. They had tiny, deep-set windows
and thick, low walls. The building materials used were
those available on the island, such as mud, stone,
driftwood and reeds for thatching. A wooden screen

Group of girls, early 1930s. Gearóid's mother is on the
extreme right and his aunt Kate is on the extreme left at
the back.

divided the interior into a bedroom and a kitchen,
with the kitchen being the bigger of the two rooms.
The floor was made of clay or beaten mud and was
often sprinkled with white sand or bedded with stone
or driftwood. Later, tarred felt replaced the thatch.

In 1838 the islanders on the Great Blasket asked a
Protestant mission for a school and an Irish teacher.
Around 1839, a Protestant group, the Dingle and

Ventry Mission, built and opened the first school on the Great Blasket, which afterwards became known as the soupers' school. Pupils were taught how to read and write in Irish. Reverend Thomas Moriarty, who was the minister at Ventry, was responsible for organising the mission's work on the Great Blasket, Dunquin and Ventry. He became the main founder of the Ventry Relief Committee, which aided the western parishes during the Great Famine. Around 1840, a house for the school's teacher was built on the Great Blasket. With its high walls, generous space and boarded floors, it set a new standard for houses on the island.

Around 1846, the school on the Great Blasket cooked its pupils a breakfast of soup and Indian meal each morning. By 1847 Indian meal was being served to all the island's children, regardless of their religion. The British Association was partly responsible for the supply. By 1848 the school had a roll call of over fifty children. As well as teaching and feeding the children, the mission gave paid employment to some men and women on the island. The work mainly involved improving and walling the landing area.

Over time, the mission claimed that at least ten families on the island had converted to its religion, but by 1850 nine of the ten converted families had reverted back to their own faith and the school closed. At that stage, the school and the teacher's house were both dilapidated. In addition, some of the breakwater

This 1937 photo was taken from a *naomhóg* as it
approached the Great Blasket harbour. Photo: John Petch.

had blown away and was later completely destroyed by
a storm. In April and November 1850, two shipwrecks
occurred. Their salvage ensured extra food supplies for
the islanders, which meant that they were no longer
reliant on Protestant aid. The Protestant influence on
the island had well and truly come to an end.

During and after the Famine, the population of
the Great Blasket fell from 153 islanders in 1841 to
97 in 1851. The Dunquin parish lost almost half of its
population during the same period.

Around 1860 a national school opened on the Great Blasket. Usually it had one resident teacher, often two. The island had no nurse, doctor, priest or shop and no place of burial for the islanders, apart from the ground at Rinn a' Chaisleáin for unbaptised babies, those who took their own lives and shipwrecked sailors.

In 1881 the population on the Great Blasket stood at 136. In 1890 the islanders were plagued with typhoid, perhaps because of poor housing conditions.

In the 1890s a boat slip and breakwater were built on the Great Blasket by the Congested Districts Board of Ireland, which was set up in 1891 to ease poverty and congested living conditions in the west of Ireland. In particular, it aimed to help poor areas by funding public works, such as piers for small ports. It also wanted to update farming methods and support local factories in order to provide employment and halt emigration.

In 1907 the Congested Districts Board bought the Great Blasket from the Earl of Cork. In 1910 the board began building houses at the top of the island. These faced east, unlike the older houses, which faced south. They were built with mixed gravel, cement and wooden boards and roofed with slate. Many of the islanders worked as labourers on the sites and got two shillings for a day's work.

As well as building, the board also changed the method of land ownership on the island. The good land that lay north of the village was fenced and

Gearóid's grandfather Ceaist (*right*) and Ceaist's nephew, Dan Eoghain Bháin (*left*), working with ropes in the mid-1930s. Courtesy of Stan Mason, photo: Thomas Mason.

divided into sixty-six fields, each of which was given to the families named in the deed of transfer of the island to the Congested Districts Board. Rent due in respect of each holding varied. One particular tenant paid seventeen shillings yearly, while his grandfather had been charged £10 in his day. Each field on the island had a name, such as An Gort Bán or An Gort Fada.

Some names were repeated several times, although these were differentiated by adding the owner's name, such as Garraí Gála Sheáin Uí Shé. Every holding included a small piece of strand. The rest of the island was designated as commonage ground and split evenly between twenty-five families. The commonage was mainly used for grazing and cutting turf. The islanders carried out certain chores together, such as sheep shearing, and animals were identified by snipped ear-markings; each family had its own particular shape of marking. By 1911 the Great Blasket had twenty-nine households and a population of 160.

In 1922, when the Irish Free State came into being, the role of the Congested Districts Board passed to the Irish Land Commission, which was set up in 1881 as a rent-fixing commission and was responsible for redistributing farmland in Ireland. It gave freehold rights to all the island families.

While the islanders lived on the Great Blasket, they passed down a rich culture and an oral craft of storytelling from generation to generation. From 1929 onwards their literary talent began to emerge, mainly due to the encouragement of scholars who visited the island, such as Carl Marstrander, Robin Flower, Brian Ó Ceallaigh, Kenneth Jackson and George Thompson. The fact that Robin Flower asked to have his ashes strewn over the highest peak of the Great Blasket shows the extent of the affection and respect the scholars had for the island and its people.

During the six-year period from 1929 to 1935, the islanders' three most famous books were published in Irish: *The Islandman* by Tomás Ó Criomhthain, *Peig* by Peig Sayers and *Twenty Years A-Growing* by Muiris Ó Súilleabháin. All three writers painted a vivid picture of the harsh realities of life on the Great Blasket, while Peig Sayers and Muiris Ó Súilleabháin also recalled the periods they spent living on the mainland. Of the three writers, Tomás Ó Criomhthain was the only one who had lived his whole life on the island, although he often stayed in Dunquin with relations, the Ó Muircheartaigh family. Seán Ó Muircheartaigh, the head of the house, was a great Irish scholar who gave Tomás his first taste of literature.

In *The Islandman*, the fact that Tomás Ó Criomhthain didn't mention the deaths of some of his children due to illness and accidents until the end of the book may come as a shock to the reader, as failing to refer to their deaths earlier seems to make light of the tragedies. A reference to Tomás in an interview given by his grandson Paddy Malone gives an insight into the author's character: 'I was told he was very tough when he was young. All the Criomhthains had it – Criomhthain toughness – pure steel. And not in body alone, in mind too. It would be hard to make them weep or shed a tear. You couldn't imagine them pining after a death. They were very hard like that.'

Perhaps the essence of all three books was best captured in the words of Tomás himself when he wrote, 'I have written minutely of much that we did, for it was my wish that somewhere there should be a memorial of it all, and I have done my best to set down the character of the people about me so that some record of us might live after us, for the like of us will never be again.'

When the island school closed at Christmas 1941, it had only six pupils on its roll call: Máirín, Liam, Máirtín and Tomás O Ceárna along with Eibhlín and Máire Ní Ghuithín. From then on, the islanders sent their children to school on the mainland.

Other factors fuelled the depopulation of the island, especially emigration. After the Second World War, many of the islanders' relatives living in America invited them over and sent money to pay for their fares. Young people began to leave in droves. And so the exodus from the Great Blasket continued until finally, those who remained had no choice but to move to the mainland.

Part 2

6

Dunquin

WE HAD BARELY SET foot in our new home in Dunquin when Mam said, 'You'll be off to school tomorrow, Gearóid.' I was not at all happy, as the school children had frightened the daylights out of me earlier that morning when we had passed by the school, hauling our belongings, on our way from the pier to our house. All the pupils were perched on the school wall and the gang of them stared hard at me, as if I had two heads. They scared me because I had never before seen so many boys and girls all bunched together in one place. School was the last place I wanted to go, as I dreaded having to face all the children again. But I had no say in the matter and was sent on my way early the following morning when the Ferriters from next door called to collect me.

The school had only one teacher, Mrs Lynch, and more than thirty pupils, all divided into eight classes

This was taken in front of Gearóid's house in Dunquin, back row (*l–r*): Gearóid's uncle Maraisín Mhuiris and Maras Mhaidhc Léan Ó Guithín; front row (*l–r*): Gearóid's father, Gearóid, Gearóid's mother and Dan Mitchell. Courtesy of Gearóid Ó Laoí.

in the same room, which was lined with two-seater desks. Mrs Lynch put me into the class for infants, all of whom were younger than me. She gave me a desk at the top, next to Páidín Kearney. She told him to take charge of me and gave Pat Ferriter the task of teaching me the alphabet. Later, when she asked me to write on the lines of my copybook, I made a few attempts but I messed up badly, as I wasn't used to writing on lines. I became upset and bawled like a baby. When I went home I told Mam that the school was full of small old people, which was my way of describing the boys and girls in the senior classes. I moaned that school was too hard.

After a few days I got the hang of it. I settled in quickly, as I was confident, sharp, good at my lessons, loved reading and had a flair for languages. We were taught how to write in English but not how to speak it, which was a shame, as that proved to be a huge drawback to me in later years. We never spoke English among ourselves, only to tourists, and they were few and far between then. Although I had no great love for maths, I coped.

By the following September I had moved up to first class, in with my own age group with Eibhlín Keane, Páidín Kearney, Máirín John Larry Kavanagh, and Seán Ferriter. From then on, when Mam bought my schoolbooks in Dingle for the following year I read the lot of them from cover to cover during the summer holidays.

During the summer holidays of 1954 I spent a lot of time with my grandfather Ceaist. By then he had eased off on work. He had gone downhill since the death of my grandmother, June Eoghain Bháin. For years he had suffered from a bad heart and I remember one night on the Great Blasket when Tom Pheaidí Mharas and Seánín Mhicil brought him in home. He was in a bad way, bent in two with pain. Yet despite the huge change of moving to Dunquin, he settled in well. He was easy-going and nothing ever fazed him. Many days, we climbed up the mountain, An Maoilinn, at the back of Dunquin for turf. He had a flair for mending fishing nets and I often sat on the step at the back of the house, watching him patch up holes. Every Saturday night, the two of us visited the Ferriters next door to listen to the radio programme *Aonach na mBailéad*, which was presented in Irish by Seán Ó Síocháin and aired ballads in Irish and English, many of them sung by Martin Dempsey, a well-known actor. We'd make ourselves snug on the sofa and Ceaist would listen with all ears to the music, as he was always on the lookout for new tunes to play on his fiddle. Once the show ended, he'd have a big chat with Tadhg and Johnnie Ó Guithín, who were uncles of the Ferriters, men of his own age, and lived in the house with the family. On Sundays we usually strolled a few miles to Coumeenole to visit his cousins, the Criomhthain family. Tiúit called to see him most nights and they chatted well into the small hours, just as they had always done on the Great Blasket.

In our house, Mam laid down the law that anyone who became ill should go to bed and stay there until they were better. In early 1955, Ceaist began to spend a lot of time in bed. One day in April, Dad came down the stairs and said, 'He's gone.'

My grandfather was laid out in a brown habit in his bedroom, in a coffin made by Seán Beoláin. He had a huge wake. Dad bought big wooden barrels of stout and currant cakes, while Mam and the neighbouring women baked white, brown and maize bread. Seán Tom Kearney stayed up all night, as it was the custom not to leave a corpse alone. Róibéard Webster, a student from Tipperary, happened to be staying with us at the time. He bunked in with me in the bedroom next to where my grandfather was waked. He kept me awake all night telling ghost stories. I didn't go to the funeral, as Mam said I was too young.

I missed not having my grandfather around. When Dad took up the fiddle for the first time after his death, hearing him play alone, without my grandfather, was the loneliest feeling in the world. Tiúit was lost without him, as they had always been the best of pals.

Soon after my grandfather's death, Mam made big changes to the house. She shopped all round her and bought everything in sight. I don't know where she got the money; maybe my grandfather had left a legacy. She never borrowed, as in those days most people thought banks should only be used by businesses and never went next or near them.

She dragged me along with her on all her shopping sprees. At the time, Dunquin was outside the bus route, so we walked four miles over the hill to Ventry and then boarded the bus to Tralee. She bought tablecloths, cutlery, ware, towels, beds, mattresses and bed linen. She also bought six washstands, which were stands with a sunken, moveable washbowl, a soap holder, a towel rack, a tall water jug and a big mirror.

Dad did a bit of shopping too. One day he came home and announced that he had booked a radio from Quilter, a radio dealer in Dingle. I couldn't sleep with the excitement, knowing we'd have top-class entertainment in our house at the turn of a button. Quilter came the next day. He marched into the kitchen carrying an aerial and a lead. I watched his every move as he fixed the aerial on the chimney, then ran the lead down from the chimney, wound it around a metal piece he had inserted in the eaves and pushed it in through a hole in the bottom part of the kitchen window. The radio had two batteries, one acid, or wet battery, and one dry battery. Quilter gave Dad clear instructions to charge the wet battery often. The dry battery had plus and minus plugs, which had to be plugged in at the back of the radio, while the wet battery had hooks. In only a matter of minutes, Quilter had the radio up and running. I leapt into the air when I heard it. The choice of stations was endless and I moved the knob excitedly from one station to another. I loved tuning in to Athlone and Hilversum, which was a popular Dutch station, as well as AFN, the American Forces Network. One of my favourite programmes was *Take the Floor*, an entertainment show presented by Din Joe on Sundays, with Irish dancing as its main feature. Dad passed on the job of recharging the wet battery to me, which meant a trip to Kruger, who had the charging equipment in his shop. I usually dropped the battery in to him on a Thursday. Whenever I called to collect it, he'd wind me up and say it wasn't ready, as he knew how much I loved that radio.

Soon after the arrival of the radio, Mam got down to the business of painting the house from top to bottom with the help of Dad, who did all the preparatory work. She painted the rooms in a variety of colours, mainly green and yellow, which were popular at the time. In the kitchen she installed a Calor Kosangas cooker and a Calor Kosangas light system, which was wired to a cylinder under the stairs. The lamp hung in the middle of the kitchen and had a glass covering to protect it from draughts. Once the mantle was lit by a match, it took fire, lit up and then glowed, bringing a certain magic and warmth to the kitchen. Its brightness could be turned high or low.

By Christmas of that year, the house had been totally revamped. It looked like a palace. Even though we had no running water, Dad managed to install a

Cáit a' Rí pictured outside her house at Baile an Teampaill in Dunquin. Cáit was known as the princess and was the sister of Mary Pheats Mhicí Uí Guithín.

flush toilet with the help of a local builder. They put a big water tank on the back kitchen, which Dad had already extended himself. They ran pipes from the top of the back kitchen down from the tank to a connection and joined a pipe from the roof of the back kitchen to the toilet system. Water flowed into the toilet system, which had the same mechanism as a flush toilet.

With the help of Dálaigh, a brother of Tom Pheaidí Mharas, Dad converted one of the outhouses into a bedroom and a living room with a kitchen area. The two rooms adjoining the kitchen were already set up as bedrooms, which meant that we then had seven bedrooms: four upstairs and three downstairs.

The year before, we had kept some relations who had come on holiday to Dunquin, among them Dad's cousin Dan Connor, who used to send him pipes from America, and his wife Mary, who was born in Baltimore. I found them loud and excited. They hired a huge automatic car, which they drove at speed around the narrow, winding roads, frightening everyone in sight. But now Mam was gearing up for even more holiday-makers, as the tourist industry in the area seemed ready to boom. Kruger had been running a guesthouse for years and others like Mam decided to give it a go, among them Julia Landers, Nancy O'Connor and Eliza Hoare as well as Mary Pheats Mhicí and her sister Kate, the princess, whom Mam always called Cáit a' Rí, which means Kate, the daughter of the king. The two of them were great pals and visited each other often.

On 31 July 1955, in the village of Gráig between Ballyferriter and Dunquin, Brú na Gráige was officially opened to accommodate male students who wished to spend the summer months among native

Gearóid at the opening of Brú na Gráige. Courtesy of
Pádraig Kennelly.

Irish speakers. Father Tadhg Ó Murchú, the priest and
teacher from Saint Finbarr's College in Cork, who had
been visiting the Great Blasket since the 1930s, was

instrumental in its foundation. Before the hostel was built he had also built a smaller house for students, An Bothán Dubh, on a site he had camped at for many years during the summer months with students, some of whom were studying for the priesthood. A farming family, the Kennedys, gave the sites for both hostels.

Brú na Gráige had a huge effect on tourism in the Dingle Peninsula. Students came from all over, such as from Clonliffe College in Dublin and Chríost Rí secondary school in Cork. The hostel placed west Kerry well and truly on the map and brought great life and fun to the area, especially as it ran *céilí* dancing nightly from June to August. During those months, my father and Seán de hÓra played there every Saturday and Sunday, which were always huge nights. Seán was a first cousin of Tom Pheaidí Mharas. He played the button accordion and sang *sean-nós*, which is a traditional style of singing. Whenever Páidín Kearney and I tagged along, Father Tadhg always gave us a bottle of bubbly white lemonade, which we loved. Until then we had never tasted white lemonade, only red. At the end of the night, he treated Dad and Seán to a bottle of stout.

Word quickly spread about Brú na Gráige and over time Dunquin became popular with tourists, many of them nuns, brothers and priests, such as Father Nessan from Rochestown College in Cork, who was big into athletics, and Father Bertie Troy, a great hurler who taught at Saint Colman's in Fermoy and went on to

manage the famous three-in-a-row Cork hurling
teams of the 1970s.

Academics came in their droves, among them men
from University College Cork, such as Pádraig Tyers
from the Irish department, who played in goal with
the Cork senior inter-county football team, Professor
Seán Ó Tuama, who played with Glen Rovers, and
the university's registrar, Jim Hurley, who had been
a freedom fighter with Tom Barry in west Cork and
hurled with Blackrock. These guys introduced me to
the sport of road bowling, which is played by throwing
a 28-ounce iron and steel ball the size of a tennis ball
along a set route on the road. The player with the least
number of shots to the finish line wins. The men played
in pairs. Páidín Kearney and I fell in with them at Gráig
and trailed them all the way to Carhue in Dunquin.
Their strength, fitness and precision fascinated me. I
watched in awe as each bowler ran along the road, gave
a short skip and jump and then hurled the bowl as far
ahead as possible, with great speed and accuracy. They
played tip rugby too on the strand and left Páidín and
myself join in. Two teams played against each other.
If a player was tipped while he had the ball, he had
to pass it. The sweat poured out through Páidín and
me, as we always gave it our best shot, even though we
were no match for any of the men, but it was a game
where the weak and the strong blended well together,
as the ball passed so quickly from one to the other and
everyone got a chance.

As well as Brú na Gráige, improvements in the roads helped drive the tourist industry. In the mid-1950s Kerry County Council started a scheme to tar the roads from Dingle to all areas of the Dingle Peninsula, as most of the terrain was rocky. The scheme required a huge workforce and provided much employment to the men in Dunquin. The road improvements attracted a better transport system and big tourist buses became more frequent around the cliff road of Slea Head.

The road trucks were everywhere. They brought a new excitement to my life and I became obsessed with them, watching their every move. I timed how long it took to tar a section of the road, as I wanted to guess how long it would be before the trucks would be tarring the stretch of road outside my house. I couldn't wait to have them working there, pouring out hot, sticky, black tar, tipping over loads of chips and rolling, with dust and noise everywhere and the smell of fresh tar. I argued with the Ferriters next door, who boasted that the trucks would reach their house before mine. I told them that the trucks would be hitting our place first, as we owned an outhouse on the bridge before their house. That shut them up. I hung around the truck drivers and flung questions at them, one after the other, until they were blue in the face from answering me. I wanted to find out what they were doing and where they were going next and how many loads of chippings a day they could collect. I became great pals with one of them, John Paul. One evening he told me to hop into his truck for a spin. I nearly burst with excitement. I was hoping the Ferriters would be around to see me, but there wasn't a trace of them. We drove to a quarry for a load of chippings and John Paul treated me to a bottle of fizzy orange on the way back. I felt full of importance pulling up in Dunquin, knowing the men would be waiting to rake and roll our load.

On a wet day the roadwork came to a halt and the men took shelter in one of our outhouses, which we named the County Council Bothán. The workers played music, sang songs and played cards. The Ferriters and I were always stuck in the middle of them. Sometimes we wished for rain, as the *craic* was so good.

During the summer months I had much fun at home too, as our house became a hive of activity. It was always bursting at the seams but Mam never turned anyone away, as she always had fierce pity for anyone who had nowhere to stay. When I got up in the morning, a stranger would often be sleeping on the floor. Once somebody ended up kipping in an outhouse.

Most of the tourists who stayed with us came from Cork, Dublin, Galway and Waterford. Mam never needed to advertise, as anyone who came to stay booked on the spot for the following year and told all their friends about us. A school inspector named

Tomas Ó Laoi as well as secondary school teachers Diarmaid Ó Donnacha and Piaras Ó Dálaigh, along with their families, came back year after year. The tourists often took me swimming with them, before and after lunch, usually to Tráigh A' Choma or Tráigh Chlochair.

One of my favourite guests was Des, a biker from Dublin, the coolest guy ever to set foot in Dunquin. He rode a massive motorbike with two huge black boxes on the back and dressed in black leather and a big helmet. One day he took me for a ride on the back of the bike, without a helmet. We zoomed at full speed all the way to Ballyferriter, our heads almost hitting the road as we whizzed round the bends. The roar and speed of the bike and the sensation of air blowing in my ears thrilled me to bits and gave me a sense of freedom and danger I had never known before. I felt fearless.

Whenever Des came to stay, two other guys came with him. One of them was Peadar, a skinny, spick-and-span civil servant who took great pride in his clothes. Des was always up to devilment and always throwing jibes at Peadar, saying all he needed was a bowler hat to finish off his prim-and-proper look. One morning when the three of us were kicking around a ball at Tráigh A' Choma, Des tried his best to give Peadar a wetting and kept pounding the ball nearer and nearer down to the sea in the hope that Peadar would fall in. By chance, my feet and Peadar's got

Gearóid and his pet donkey in Dunquin in the 1950s.
Courtesy of Donal MacMonagle/macmonagle.com

entangled in a tackle and he fell flat on his back just
as a massive wave rolled in. Des and I were in stitches
seeing Peadar drenched to the bone and his clothes
sopping wet. 'You're like a drowned rat,' Des laughed,
thrilled at the state of him.

Mam worked hard seven days a week, non-stop, to cater for the summer tourists. In the morning she dished them up a hot breakfast. In the middle of the day she served dinner, usually soup, chops and vegetables or stew, followed by a dessert of jelly and ice cream or trifle. She served tea bang on six o'clock. I washed the pots and dug the potatoes. Apart from that, she did it all on her own.

Dad turned into a night owl and stayed up half the night playing his fiddle and entertaining the guests, who danced gaily to his tunes. In those times, music was played for dancers and was never played merely for listeners. Holiday-makers from other guesthouses poured in too, as well as from Kruger's bar, which he had built onto the shop. They joined in the set dancing and step dancing or played a few tunes. One guy from Cork landed with a guitar. Dad had bumped into him in Dingle and invited him home when he heard he had nowhere to stay. The man was a giant and had to bend down every time he walked under the gas lamp in the kitchen. It was my first time seeing a guitar and I couldn't wait to hear how it sounded. One night a pretty Wicklow girl in her late teens popped in and started step dancing. Soon a crowd gathered, but everyone let her have the floor as she dazzled them with her steps. I couldn't take my eyes off her. It was the first time I had ever looked twice at a girl. Later some of the crowd joined her and they danced a Kerry set. From June to August, I never once put my head on my pillow without hearing the strains of music blasting up from below and the rhythmic pounding of feet on the floor.

Like us, Mary Pheats Mhicí kept tourists, among them the teacher and writer Risteard Ó Glaisne, who had been one of her regular guests on the Great Blasket. Every morning, when he drove to Ballyferriter for the paper, he took me with him for the spin. On the way home, on a straight stretch between Gráig and Dunquin, he'd give me the wheel, sit back and pretend to read his paper. 'Okay, Gearóid, drive on,' he'd say to me. 'You'll make a great rally driver some day.' My head would swell, as I had been fascinated with cars ever since I had travelled with Mam in Daniel Kane's lush taxi, with its shiny leather seats. That journey from Dunquin to Graffies was my first memory of ever sitting in a car, and its power to whizz past everything in sight left me gobsmacked.

Another frequent visitor to Dunquin was the poet Seán Ó Ríordáin, whom I liked a lot, especially as he often treated me to a thick slice of vanilla ice cream with a crunchy wafer at either side. He reminded me of Risteard and Mary Pheats Mhici's other annual guests on the island, as he was a kind, quiet, refined man. He drove a small black Ford, wore a hat and always had a pipe dangling from his mouth. Like Risteard, he took me with him when he drove to Ballyferriter for the paper, maybe because I came from the Great Blasket, as he had great time for the islanders, especially for the writer and storyteller Peig Sayers and her son Maidhc Pheig, whom he often visited.

Another popular visitor to Dunquin was a Cork man we named An Fear Bodhar, as he was partly deaf and wore a hearing aid with a long string hanging down, which always amused me. A quiet, gentle guy, he rode a motorbike and always wore a long, belted trench coat and a beret, which added a sense of mystery to him and made him look like a spy. Years later, we found out he had, in fact, been a dispatch rider during the War of Independence.

One day after Dad had a load of gravel delivered to our house, he took the lorry driver to Kruger's for a drink. I went along too. The writer Brendan Behan happened to be sitting at the counter, as he and his wife often stayed at Kruger's. Dad had just bought me a bottle of lemonade when Brendan came over to me. He knew who I was, shook my hand, gave me a cigarette, called Kruger for a glass of stout and said, 'Gearóid, remember now that Brendan Behan gave you your first cigarette and glass of stout.'

Another famous visitor to Dunquin was the composer and musician Seán Ó Riada, who later became regarded as perhaps the most influential person in the revival of Irish traditional music. He rented a house in Clochar, near Ballyferriter, and commuted to Cork and Dublin. His presence attracted huge interest, as he was highly respected. He often played sessions with my father and Seán de hÓra, usually in our house or in Brú na Gráige. Dad was very fond of him and applied to take part in a fiddle competition Seán had organised on his weekly radio show, *Fleadh Cheoil an Raidió*. Seán drove him to Dublin, put him up for a few days and introduced him to all the Ceoltóirí Chualann musicians. Although Dad didn't win the competition, he felt proud to have taken part and had nothing but praise for Seán and the great hospitality he showed. Dad was quiet and not the least bit boastful, but he often mentioned the trip, as it must have been a huge occasion for him and one he always treasured. Coincidentally, the winner of the fiddle competition was Dad's namesake, Seán Keane, who later became famous as a member of Ceoltóirí Chualann and the Chieftains. When Seán Ó Riada moved to Cúil Aodha, Dad and Seán de hÓra were hugely disappointed, as they felt west Kerry needed a person of his calibre to inject more music and culture into the local area.

The well-known politician Seán Mac an tSaoi and his wife spent many summers in Dunquin, along with their daughter, the famous Irish language scholar, poet and writer, Máire Mhac an tSaoi. Máire's uncle, the mathematician and classical scholar Monsignor Pádraig de Brún, often stayed with the family at their holiday home, An Tigh Dubh, near Saint Gobnait's well. One year, during the last two weeks of school before the summer break, our teacher Mrs Lynch invited Máire along to teach us. We all fell head over heels in love with her. She taught us outside and we felt as if we were already on our summer holidays, with the warm sun beaming down on us and the birds singing sweetly overhead. She fuelled our imagination and swept us off to another age with tales about Celtic warriors such as Cuchulainn and Fionn and the Fianna. When she asked each one of us to say a poem, I stood up and recited '*An Gleann inar Tógadh mé*' at the top of my voice. She beamed with delight and applauded so much that my head began to swell. Then, when she asked me for a song, I hopped up again and belted out '*Amhrán na Leabhar*'.

All in all, the tourists gave me a good outlook on life. After spending only a short while in their midst, their ways and sunny nature rubbed off on me. Mixing with them was pure magic, as they brought a certain sparkle and vibrancy to Dunquin, which made me want to be like them when I grew up. I wanted to travel too, go on holiday, see many places, have fun and dress well, as to me tourists always looked as if they were dressed in their Sunday best, unlike the locals, who wore their good clothes only on a Sunday or on a special occasion and never seemed to have time to laze around. They were always chasing their tails, working from morning till night with little to show for it, trying to feed their big families and always worrying about the weather, saving their crops and the price they might get for their calves or lambs. It was sheer drudgery with no reward. The tourists did their best for them and often chipped in to help save the hay or draw in the turf. For me, living in Dunquin was great fun and I had no wish to go back to the Great Blasket. The thought never even crossed my mind, even though I was reminded of the island every day, as I could see it from our back garden.

While most of the locals welcomed the tourists with open arms, some of the islanders and others looked on them as a mixed blessing, as most of the people of Dunquin were quiet, shy people who weren't used to mixing with strangers and rarely socialised apart from visiting each other or meeting at the creamery, outside the church after Mass or at Kruger's. Then, of course, there were the begrudgers who were not at all keen on tourists flocking to Dunquin. They called the tourists 'the Lá Breas', as most of the visitors had no Irish apart from being able to say *lá brea*, which means a fine day. The begrudgers had no time for them and whined, 'They're here on their holidays and their income is rising.' But those making money on the tourist trade ignored the begrudgers and got on with the business of keeping the tourists happy and making sure they came back again. It demanded constant hard work, with early mornings and late nights.

Kruger was top dog and could cater for the tourists' every need. He kept loads of foreigners, mainly from Germany, Wales and Scotland. He sold Dunquin to them as a pretty little village at the foot of a mountain, far away from civilisation. He made good use of me to entertain them. If he was serving tourists when I walked into his shop, he'd put on a posh American twang and shout, holding out his two hands, 'Well, look who it is. This is the loneliest boy in the world, the last native child of the Great Blasket. Come on in, Gearóid, until they get a good look at you.' Then he'd grab a camera from one of the tourists and order, 'Everyone stand in there for a photo with the loneliest boy in the world, who made headlines in every country you can name because he had nobody to play with, only the seagulls. Stand on that box there, Gearóid, and say cheese.' I felt like a performing monkey and couldn't wait to escape. But Kruger was a natural. He glorified himself at all costs. He oozed confidence and knew well the power of chat, charm and advertising. And everyone knew him, from far and near. He made sure of that. He drove around west Kerry in his van with his name in big print, advertising his guesthouse. But he went further afield too.

On 26 September 1954, Kruger, my father, Faeilí, Seán de hÓra and Jerry Garvey all packed into Kruger's van and headed for Croke Park in Dublin to watch Kerry take on Meath in the All-Ireland football final. Size wise, the van was small and three of the men squashed into the back, which Kruger had laid with a mattress. Another sat in front with Kruger, whose big, bulky frame took up most of the steering space. Kerry lost by six points and my father came home crippled after the hours spent going and coming, crushed to

bits in the back of Kruger's van. He said it had been a
pilgrimage and spent the rest of the week in bed. He
brought home rosary beads, maybe for his sins, and a
match programme, which he gave to me. I treasured
that programme like nothing else I ever owned. I
became obsessed with Gaelic football, so much so that
it took over my life completely. My head was filled with
nothing but thoughts of football and an ambition to
play for Kerry. I was seven years of age.

In Kruger's shop, sweets soon stopped being the
main draw for me. Instead of going in to buy some
jellies or bulls-eyes, I went in to look at a big John
Player's calendar hanging on the wall, showing a group
of Dublin and Kerry players rising up to catch the
ball in the 1955 football All-Ireland final. I stared at
it open-mouthed, fascinated by the dropping ball. I
couldn't wait for the end of the year, when I would
ask Kruger for the calendar and take it home to hang
over my bed.

My idol became Tadghie Lyne, who played with
a club in Killarney, Dr Crokes, and scored six points
in the 1955 All-Ireland final, in which Kerry was
victorious. Whenever Mam brought home *The
Kerryman*, I snatched hold of it straight away. It was
like gold to me, as its sports reporter, Pat Foley, who
was known as PF, always wrote about the star quality
of Tadghie on the field and described in detail how
he kicked each and every point. Any time I read PF's
reports on Tadghie, my admiration for him soared

even more and he grew a few inches taller. The reports always carried photographs taken during the games. I cut out every single report and picture of Tadghie and stored them in a tin box under my bed. My uncle Maraisín Mhuiris went to a lot of matches. He told me that Tadghie was the first player he ever saw who scored a goal by kicking the ball over his head. That drove me berserk. I wanted to master the skill too and spent hour after hour, every day of the week, at the gable end of the house, trying to kick a ball over my head. Sometimes Páidín Kearney joined me.

When Cork beat Kerry in the Munster football final of 1956, Páidín and I were gutted. To add salt to our wounds, Pádraig Tyers crawled past us on the road with a car full of students from Saint Finbarr's College in Cork, blasting the horn continuously, grinning from ear to ear and the lot of them chanting, 'We are the champions.' We put down a terrible summer, listening to the Cork crowd crowing, as there was always a fierce rivalry between us.

Early that summer Mam told me I would soon be getting a new baby sister or brother. I paid little heed as I was a free spirit, living in my own world. Some months before, Mam had stopped going to Mass, which was the tradition then, as pregnant women kept a low profile in the latter stages of pregnancy. When she went into labour in the middle of the night, Dad dashed off for Kruger and the three of them took off for Dingle hospital, with the noise from Kruger's exhaust waking half the parish and leaving a cloud of smoke behind.

That evening, as I lazed in the sun with Seán Ferriter in a field behind his house, Dad called me, waving a telegram in his hand. With excitement written all over his face, he told me I had a new baby sister. When I heard the news, I felt a new adventure lay ahead, that times would change, and I was curious to know what exactly would happen.

When Dad and I went to the hospital I expected to find Mam looking poorly. Instead, she looked gorgeous, as she glowed with happiness and was all dolled up with lipstick and pearls, which she loved. When I saw my baby sister in a cot beside her, I said, 'Máirín Kearney's doll is bigger than her.' Mam named her Ann Marie.

Once they came home, I was put in my place and told to stay quiet and not to disturb Ann Marie, who was wrapped snugly in a shawl and put into a pram by the fire. Mam taught me how to put Ann Marie to sleep by rocking her in the pram. One day in the back garden, I rocked the pram so hard it toppled over. Mam gave me a fine hiding across the calves of my legs with a sopping dishrag, which she always seemed to have handy. But I dared not cry for fear of another onslaught, as I had been warned to stay quiet.

As time went on I became attached to Ann Marie, who had a head of beautiful black hair and plump cheeks. But by the autumn I felt peeved, as I knew I was no longer the main attraction. So I packed a bag and left, along with Máirín Ferriter, whose reason for running away I can't recall. We walked as far as Carhue, where we bumped into Seán Connor, a local. He persuaded us to turn around and go home. After that, I accepted my lot and stayed put.

In January 1957, Martin Houlihan, who used to serve Mass and act as the church clerk, died. Soon afterwards, Father Harrington, the temporary curate in Ballyferriter, came to the school and said that he wanted to train some boys for the altar. He chose Seán and Páidín Kearney, Pat Ferriter and me. We would be the first altar boys in Dunquin. He mustn't have known that we were always messing at Mass, pinning strips of paper onto the back of people's coats or onto their trousers, then laughing our heads off as they walked up piously to the altar to receive communion. We lived in hope that the men would tear the arse out of their trousers when they got up after kneeling at the altar.

Every single day without fail, Father Harrington popped into the school to teach us altar service and pump us with Latin phrases, which we picked up fast enough. Some days he marched us up to the church, where he said Mass and we practised the responses. Most days, the four of us strolled up and down the roads and recited parts of the Mass, such as *dominus vobiscum*, which means the Lord be with you.

One day, when a local smart aleck overheard us, he answered us in Irish: 'He's gone east the village.' I looked on it as an affront to our social standing in the village, as by then I'd become cocky and was full of myself, convinced I was better than most, being one of the chosen few in the village and able to speak some Latin. Our first time serving together on the altar at 11 a.m. Mass on a Sunday went off without a hitch, but soon after we made a holy show of ourselves.

As it happened, Seán Ferriter and I were always squabbling and pulling and tugging at each other. One time we ended up in a stream and nearly tore each other asunder, while the other two lads stayed on the bank, laughing their heads off. We were always at each other's throats, no matter where we were, so sooner or later, it was inevitable that our enmity would rear its ugly head on the altar.

Our soutanes always hung in the same place in the sacristy. But unbeknownst to me, one Sunday morning before Mass, Seán switched mine with a longer one. When the four of us paraded onto the altar, dressed in our black soutanes, white surplices and black canvas shoes, I noticed my soutane trailed after me and looked about four inches too long. I took extra care walking, especially when the time came for me to move the missal from one side of the altar to the other so that the priest could read the gospel.

Lifting my soutane off the floor, I walked slowly up the three steps of the altar, on the right-hand side, and collected the missal. As I had to hold the book with both hands, I couldn't lift my soutane again when I walked down. But I took my time and managed to move down the three steps without a blip. Then I carefully genuflected in front of the altar, moved to the left and began to walk up the steps again. Just as I was about to put my foot on the third step, I tripped and myself and the missal flew head-first towards the sacristy. The whole congregation broke their sides laughing. Later, Father Harrington asked me, 'Were you in Kruger's before you came?' I knew Seán was the culprit and vowed to get him back.

On the morning Seán had charge of ringing the bell on the altar, I decided to strike. I went to the church early and loosened the screws on the top of the bell. All through Mass, I had a big smirk off my face. I waited impatiently for the fun to begin. The consecration came and Seán struck the bell once. It stayed intact. But when he hit the bell a second time, he blew off the top and watched, aghast, as it went flying against the wall, making an almighty clatter and causing the congregation to erupt in laughter once again.

Another morning, while the four of us were perched on the steps of the altar listening to Father Kissane's sermon, a local man in the second row caught my attention. He had a bad twitch in his eye. The more I watched him, the faster he started to blink. I got a fit of giggling and couldn't stop. When the other lads spotted me, they started off. After Mass, Mam was waiting for me at the church gate with a cross face on her. She gave me a right telling off. At least she didn't have the dishrag handy.

In the spring, I got a huge surprise. For a long time the weather had been harsh and cold and the village was riddled with mumps, measles, earaches and colds. I had longed for snow ever since I first saw Christmas postcards from America showing cities and towns under an avalanche of snow. Each night I put my ear to the radio, listened to the weather forecast and prayed for some snow to come our way. One night I heard the magic words, 'a likelihood of snow'.

The next morning I rose at the crack of dawn. I couldn't believe the sight before me. The whole village and all the fields were gleaming white and thick flakes of snow were still falling, heavily and silently. Mam said the school would be closed and told me to stay at home, but I insisted on going as I wanted to plough my way through the blizzard and pelt everyone with snowballs. When I walked into the schoolyard there wasn't a soul to be seen, only Mrs Lynch, all wrapped up in a heavy coat, cap and gloves. Rubbing her hands together, she said, 'There's no school today, Gearóid, and there won't be any for a week.' I shuffled my way back home and called in for Páidín Kearney. We just stood together in the middle of the road, gazing around in wonder, mesmerised by the dazzling whiteness. Then we took to the fields with the rest of the Kearneys and spent hours making snowmen, one after the other, until we had snowmen of all shapes and sizes standing in every nearby field, with stones inserted for their eyes and carrots for their noses.

One evening, after a few days of snowfall, I got a bright idea. Páidín and I peeped in our kitchen window to make sure nobody was around. Then we sneaked in and grabbed hold of the tin bathtub in front of the fire, which the family bathed in every Saturday night for Mass the following morning. We hauled it by its two handles, dragged it over the ditch and pulled it up to the top of a slippery, wet field behind our house. Then Páidín and I took it in turns to hop inside and slide down the field, as fast as if we were on a snowy slope on the Alps. Hours went by. Bedtime came and went, but we couldn't tear ourselves away from the fun. I got the fright of my life when Mam appeared at the ditch, waving a soaking dish cloth. She threatened to give me a fine lash of it if I didn't get quickly inside, adding, 'And bring that bathtub with you.'

In summer, Páidín and I often teamed up with Pádraig Breathnach, whose father Risteard was a professor of Irish at University College Cork. The family came to Dunquin every year and stayed in their caravan at Bóthar na hAbhann, near Kruger's. Unlike Páidín and me, Pádraig got pocket money every week. He spent most of it on cigarettes, as he loved smoking. One summer he took it upon himself to show Páidín and me the joys of nicotine. We spent three solid days behind the school with him, trying to master the art of inhaling a non-tip cigarette and nearly choking in the process, throwing up and becoming weary from listening to him mocking us. But he was hell-bent on making smokers of us and kept feeding us cigarettes until we learned how to draw in the smoke. Since that first day I inhaled a bloody cigarette, I've never stopped smoking. Once I started, I became a thief and often nicked a Player's cigarette from my mother's box. If she knew her packet was going down faster than before, she never let on.

Mártan Beag Ó Catháin, a cousin who lived nearby, was another buddy of mine. His mother had been an only child and she was known as 'the baby'. A kind woman, she always gave our family eggs and milk when our cows went dry or the hens stopped laying. Mártan and I spent hours playing on the earth outside his house, which we mapped out as a copy of Dunquin, with the main road and all its winding, hilly side roads. Like me, Mártan loved cars and we kept a collection of stones of all shapes and sizes, each one looking a lot like cars we had seen in the village. We pretended the stones were cars and raced them along the earth with our hands. We whizzed along the tracks, driving at full speed around hairpin bends, never braking. Then we spun the cars around full circle and zoomed off the opposite way, often crashing into an oncoming car and blasting it off the road.

Once a week, when a lorry drove into the village to deliver goods such as maize, flour and coal, it raised a hell of a lot of dust. Mártan and I tried to whip up more dust than the lorry. We tied bunches of hedging around our waist and raced up and down the road yelling, with the bushes hitting the ground behind us and the dust flying in every direction. While milking, Dan Mitchell, whom we called Dangle, used to leave his milk churns outside on the road with the tops off. His hefty wife would chase after us as we ran by, waving a big stick at us and swearing to tell our parents about our blackguarding.

Mártan and I said Mass too in his back garden, on a table set up as an altar. Taking off the priests came naturally, as we were surrounded by them – old priests and young priests as well as young seminarians, all dressed in black. The villagers put them on a pedestal. The local men tipped their caps to salute them and the women danced attendance on them, filling them up with pots of tea and stuffing them with stacks of homemade cakes. We aspired to being one of them and stood behind the garden altar giving sermons out loud and scolding the make-believe congregation in front of us for their awful, unforgivable sins.

We tuned in to all the hurling matches on the radio and tried to imitate Mícheál Ó Hehir's lively commentary by using all his catchy phrases to describe bends, strikes and lifts. We played hurling with Mam's butter bats and tried to score goals by pounding a ball in between two stones. I was always John Doyle of Tipperary or Nicky Rackard of Wexford, while

Mártan had to be Tipperary hurlers Jimmy Doyle or Donie Nealon. Eddie Campion – a Kilkenny man who was married to the schoolteacher's daughter, Máirín – used to watch us playing. One day he came along with two hurleys and *sliotars* for us. We were away with it then. But football was still our number one. It was always on our minds.

We looked forward to *The Kerryman* newspaper every week, which Mam brought from Dingle if she went shopping there. Otherwise we got hold of it on a Friday night, when Timmy McCarthy, a baker in Dingle, drove into Dunquin in his van with a delivery of bread, cakes and newspapers. We flicked through it quickly until we found PF's football report, which always gave us a huge lift. Before every game, he described each player's strengths and weaknesses in detail, so much so that we thought we knew every player personally. His report always carried pictures of the players in action and we feasted our eyes on them, spellbound by the men's physique and skill. From then until Sunday, we talked about nothing only the game ahead.

One of the players, our local hero Tom Long, featured often in PF's reports. Tom lived in Ventry and played senior football with Kerry. One morning we couldn't believe our luck when Tom came to the parish to save hay with his brother Maidhc. Mártan and I camped ourselves in the hay field for the day and studied him from head to toe. 'Look at his muscles,' said Mártan. 'He can pike hay twice as fast as Maidhc.' In our minds, he was ten feet tall and a mile wide and we sat there for hours, enthralled.

On 2 June 1957, a scorching Whit bank holiday Sunday, the day of the first round of the Munster football at Walsh Park in Waterford, Mártan, Páidín Kearney and I felt cock-sure that Kerry would beat Waterford, no bother. Waterford had great hurlers, but when it came to football, we knew they weren't a patch on Kerry.

It was the longest, hottest day Mártan, Páidín and I ever spent, hanging around the road, knowing we'd have to wait until ten o'clock that night for the result to be announced on the radio on *Gaelic Sports Results*. We had no other way of finding out the score. Any time we went home, we were heckled by four guys from Waterford who happened to be staying in our house.

At five minutes to ten o'clock, we all gathered in the new kitchen to tune in to Seán Óg Ó Ceallacháin with the sports results. The Waterford boys rubbed their hands together in anticipation and one of them gloated, 'Our time has come.' But Páidín, Mártan and I never rose to the bait. We held our cool, as we knew Waterford had no chance on earth of winning. Ten minutes later, Seán Óg began his report of the day's matches, with the winning teams always being called out first. Páidín, Mártan and I couldn't wait to celebrate. Then we heard Seán Óg announce, 'Munster championship senior football, first round, Waterford two goals and five points, Kerry ten points.' We died on the spot. Being beaten by Cork in 1956 was bad enough, but being destroyed by Waterford – we just couldn't take it. Life was no longer worth living. Our whole summer was ruined, gone in a flash. We never recovered.

In the late 1950s, when word spread that *The Playboy of the Western World* was being shot on Inch Strand, a huge crowd of tourists of all nationalities swarmed around Dunquin, mainly to get a glimpse of the film's leading lady, Siobhán McKenna, who played the role of Pegeen Mike, the character Synge based on Mary Pheats Mhicí. During the shoot, Siobhán stayed at Kruger's, along with her actor husband, Denis O'Dea, and their dark-haired son, Donnacha. She was a big woman, with flaming-red hair and captivating eyes. Kruger was stone mad about her and waited on her hand and foot, bowing at the sight of her. Every morning a big, posh, chauffeur-driven car pulled up outside his guesthouse to whisk Siobhán and her husband off to the set. I became great buddies with Donnacha, whom Siobhán adored. He was about my age and we spent hours every day paddling and kicking a ball on the strand. In later years, Donnacha became famous when he swam for Ireland in the 1968 Summer Olympics and won a World Series of Poker bracelet in 1998.

On 8 December 1958, Peig Sayers died at Saint Elizabeth's hospital in Dingle. I had often visited her

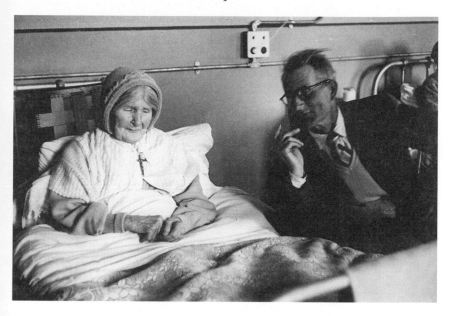

Peig Sayers and her son Maidhc in Dingle Hospital in the
1950s. Photo: Tomás Ó Muircheartaigh.

there with Mam any time we shopped in the town.
Although Peig was blind then, she always looked
bright and strong. She had a regal air about her, which
reminded me of Mary Pheats Mhici's sister Kate, the
princess. She was a lovable, cheerful character with
a big, broad face, lovely skin and a deep, clear voice,
well suited to storytelling. And she had great facial
expression, as her whole face lit up when she spoke.
When we visited her in hospital she usually sat up on
the bed, all decked out in a knitted bed-jacket and a

wool bonnet, with rosary beads in her hands, a big, shiny crucifix on her chest and a box of snuff on her locker. She often called me up beside her and held my hand. Sometimes Mam laughed aloud and recalled that when she was a young girl on the Great Blasket, Peig had often frightened the life out of her and her pals with her ghost stories, so much so that they were always scared walking home at night after listening to her. Mam always had great time for Peig and once said, 'She was a great, steady woman. She was never a gossiper.'

Another of Peig's regular visitors to the hospital had been the poet Seán Ó Ríordáin, who said, 'Her heart was as light as a starling's. Although bed-ridden and blind, she possessed more light than any in her company. I only heard her complain once. She said she felt trapped because she could not escape her own thoughts.' All of the islanders spoke well of her too and remembered her kindness to them on the Great Blasket, when she would welcome them into her home to play cards and give them Saint Bruno flake-cut tobacco to make cigarettes. Perhaps one of the nicest tributes paid to her came from Professor Seán Ó Tuama, who described her as 'a poet at heart'.

Peig's remains were brought to Saint Gobnait's church in Dunquin and I served at her funeral Mass, along with Seán and Páidín Kearney and Pat Ferriter. It was a big affair, a concelebrated Mass, with all the priests dressed in black. Father Tadhg Ó Murchú gave the sermon. He knew Peig well, ever since she lived on the Great Blasket, and acknowledged her vast legacy of folklore, which is now housed at University College Dublin. Her passion for storytelling from the time she was a young girl is recalled in her own words: 'I never had any interest in music or dancing. I'd rather listen to the old people telling stories and discussing life than listen to the sweetest music on earth.'

Although those of us who knew her will always remember Peig as a cheerful person, she suffered much tragedy during her life and lost five of her eleven children. Yet she seemed to have found a way of lifting her spirits and moving on, as described by Seosamh Ó Dálaigh, who collected hundreds of tales from her: 'She once told me about her son falling off the cliff and how his body was brought home to her, maimed and battered. As she was telling me, the tears began to fall. Then, she clapped her hands like this and her mood changed. She continued her story without any trace of sadness after that. You'd think that when she clapped her hands, she dispelled the sorrow.'

After her passing, Peig's son Maidhc Pheig must have been broken-hearted, as he had always adored her. Páidín Kearney and I often called to him in his small cottage in Dunquin. The house had a kitchen and two other rooms. It stood at the foot of Mount Eagle, at Baile Bhiocáire, next door to Seán Pheats Tom Kearney. Maidhc Pheig was nice, but too quiet for our liking, not at all entertaining. We looked on him as being a bit of an oddity. Years later, when I read Peig's autobiography, I felt it failed to reflect her jovial character and wondered if its bleak tone was due to Maidhc Pheig's input.

As well as visiting Maidhc Pheig, I had a lot of contact with all the other islanders, especially those who had lived on the island during my time there. Every Sunday morning, Tiúit popped into our house before Mass and strolled to the church with my father. He often called at night too to chat to Dad, mainly about fishing and sheep shearing. The two of them would gaze into the fire while they talked and I'd sit in the middle of them, listening to their banter and flicking through my cowboy books, which Mam always bought me in Dingle. Tiúit was a great talker and storyteller and sometimes recalled with gusto the times he struggled for survival in the middle of the sea in horrendous squalls. As the night went on, the squalls got bigger. He lived beside my grandfather, Maras Mhuiris, in a draughty old farmhouse too big for one person and drew the old-age pension. He kept goats, cut turf, rowed to the Great Blasket and Inis Tuaisceart with my father and others to tend to the sheep and spent his nights visiting neighbours or chatting in Kruger's. His companions were mainly the islanders, the people he had known all his life. Somehow, I felt his heart was still on the Great Blasket and that he would have liked to see out the end of his days there.

Seánín Mhicil (*left*) and Peaidí Mhicil (*right*) fetching
a load of turf in Dunquin in the late 1960s. Courtesy of
Maria Simonds-Gooding.

Maidhc Faight and his sister Mary lived in an old
cottage at Carhue. They cut turf, saved hay, sowed oats
and grew vegetables. They seemed happy enough and
kept to themselves, as they were quiet, especially Mary.
Apart from going to Dingle to shop sometimes, they
rarely went outside the village.

My grandfather Maras Mhuiris, Seán Mhicil, Mary
Pheats Mhicí, Peaidí Mharas Ó Dálaigh and their
families all lived in the new, small, stone, slate-roofed
cottages in Dunquin built especially for them in an
unsheltered area at Baile na Rátha. Each house had

Maras Mhaidhc Léan pictured in his house in Baile na Rátha in Dunquin with his mother's dresser from the Great Blasket in the background. Photo: Liam Blake, © *The Sound of Waves*, Real Ireland Design, 2005.

a kitchen, a scullery and three rooms. The buildings looked horrible. They were badly constructed and built block on block, with no cavity and no insulation. They were riddled with dampness. In winter, the cold in those houses was unbearable and the bedclothes were usually dripping wet. The families' main source of heat was turf and most of them kept a donkey to carry it home.

Mary Pheats Mhicí and her sons, Seán Mhaidhc Léan and Maras Mhaidhc Léan, owned a small plot of ground around their house, at the top half of the village. The land was flat and was much easier to farm than the hilly fields of the Great Blasket. The family kept a cow, sowed oats, grew vegetables and saved hay. Seán Mhaidhc Léan and Maras Mhaidhc Léan continued to fish, mainly for mackerel and lobster, and tended to their sheep on the Great Blasket. They seemed pleased with the move and Seán Mhaidhc Léan once said, 'We knew that we would all have to leave sooner or later. We couldn't leave it too late either. Soon, I'd be too old to leave. If we didn't leave then, we wouldn't have been relocated. We left when we got the chance. We didn't know how easy life could be until we left. If you wanted to plough on the mainland, you'd use a tractor. The work was far easier than it was on the island. We couldn't use a scythe to reap oats. We didn't even have a harrow.' His life on the island must have been tough, as he had to take on a man's work from the age of twelve, when his father died. When he spoke about the other islanders, he said, 'They had to leave the island – only two *naomhóg* crews left.' Although Seán Mhaidhc Léan was happy to be on the mainland, his heart may have still been on the Great Blasket. 'The island is always in my mind and so are the people who lived there. I remember the mackerel season and how delighted the children would be at that time. I remember the different chores we had to do, tillage, sowing potatoes and oats.'

Life for his mother, Mary Pheats Mhicí, was much the same as it had been on the Great Blasket. She still kept tourists, among them the annual guests who had stayed with her on the island. She kept students too, mostly from Gael Linn. Usually Pádraig Tyers arranged their holiday, as he held the post of organiser with the association.

Seán Mhicil Ó Súilleabháin, his wife June Mháire Eoghain and their sons Seánín Mhicil, Peaidí Mhicil and Maidhc Mhicil lived next door to Mary Pheats Mhicí. They kept a cow, set vegetables, sowed oats, cut turf, saved hay and fished for lobster and mackerel. Peaidí Mhicil was an out-and-out loner and loved going back to the Great Blasket to tend to the sheep. Seánín Mhicil was more outgoing, maybe because of his music, and played at Kruger's every Sunday night. Whenever the brothers strolled through the village together, they always walked in single file, one behind the other, which was the way the islanders had always walked on the Great Blasket due to the narrow pathways. The brother in front kept looking over his shoulder to talk to the brother behind. They quickly became a source of fun for the villagers, who used to laugh on seeing them and say, 'Here comes Seánín Mhicil, so Peaidí Mhicil is sure to be close behind.' Their mother, June Mháire Eoghain, passed away in the late 1950s.

Gearóid and his grandfather Maras Mhuiris outside his grandfather's house in Dunquin in the 1950s. Courtesy of Donal MacMonagle/macmonagle.com

Mam's mother also died in the late 1950s. My grandfather Maras Mhuiris became more isolated then and rarely went outside, as he was old, stooped and crippled with pain after a lifetime of hard, physical work hauling boats, animals, timber and fish. His son Maraisín Mhuiris kept the house in ship-shape condition. Just like Mam, he was highly organised and a dinger on cleanliness. The house always smelled of fresh bread, which he baked every day. He could dish up a meal fit for a king, no bother, and once I'd spot him hopping off the bus from Dingle, I'd dash straight to my grandfather's house, knowing that Maraisín Mhuiris would have brought home some tasty food, such as sausages, rashers and black and white pudding, which he'd fry up in no time. He was more refined in his ways than Faeilí, maybe because he had been in the army and had mixed more with people outside the locality. But Faeilí was still my favourite uncle. The brothers kept a cow and continued to fish, cut turf, save hay, sow oats and tend to their sheep on the Great Blasket.

In 1958 Faeilí married a local girl from Clochar, Bríde de hÓra, who was related to Seán de hÓra. Páidín Kearney and I had the task of going from door to door in the village to tell everyone to come to the ceremony at Ballyferriter church and then to the breakfast in Daniel Keane's pub. Faeilí wore a dark suit and a white shirt and Bríde wore a skirt and jacket, or a costume, as it was called then. After the breakfast everyone headed to Kruger's, but Páidín and I were fed up with the celebrations by then and so we traipsed off home.

A group of island men near the cliff top in Dunquin on a
Sunday or a wedding day. Back row (*l–r*): Maras Mhaidhc
Léan Ó Guithín, unknown and Seán Sheáisí; middle row
(*l–r*): Tom Pheaidí Mharas Ó Dálaigh, Seánín Mhicil,
Maidhc Laighin Ó Guithín, Neoidin, unknown, unknown
and unknown; front row (*l–r*): Peaidí Mharas Ó Dálaigh,
unknown, unknown, unknown, Faeilí and Seán Fillí.

Peaidí Mharas Ó Dálaigh and his sons Peaidí Beag
and Tom Pheaidí Mharas settled well enough. They
cut turf, set vegetables, sowed oats, saved hay and were
always busy sawing and chipping wood, as they were

still master carpenters and boat makers. They spent much time mending a damaged *naomhóg* or making a new one. Every summer they rowed to Inis Mhicileáin and lived there for a few weeks to tend to their sheep. Tom still played the fiddle, but mainly at home. Peaidí Mharas died in the late 1950s.

Like the rest of the islanders who had moved to Dunquin, Mam and Dad were busy too, not only with hosting and entertaining tourists, but with other work as well. In summer Dad lived on the Great Blasket for three or four weeks at a time to look after his sheep. He often rowed to Inis Tuaisceart too, along with Tiúit, Faeilí and Seán Pheats Tom Kearney, to tend to the sheep there, operating in the same way as when we had lived on the Great Blasket. He kept cattle, a donkey and a few cows, saved hay, cut turf, sowed oats and set vegetables. I helped him spread the fertilizer for the potatoes, as we needed a good supply of potatoes in early summer for the tourists. He fished for lobster, mainly with Seán Pheats Tom Kearney. Together they bought a new *naomhóg* from Bord Iascaigh Mhara for £25. When they finished their partnership, Dad kept the *naomhóg* and teamed up with Tomás Neoidin and Séamus Pound Ó Lúing, who was known as Pound. They used the boat for fishing and for rowing tourists over and back to the Great Blasket in the summer months for a day trip. Although Dad owned the boat, he split all the profit evenly with the other two men.

Dunquin

Once we had settled in Dunquin, Mam never looked back. She always had a positive outlook on life and always said people have to move on to better things. One evening when she was chatting to a tourist about the island, I heard her say, 'We had to leave. There was hardly anybody left. We were depending on *naomhógs* to bring us in and out. Bad weather often made the crossings impossible. We left because it was difficult to live where there were so few people. It was hard to live there without a school. We were sad leaving the island, but the people in Dunquin were welcoming.'

Mam still kept chickens and made butter. She started keeping turkeys too, like a lot of other women in the village who had been encouraged by the local creamery to join the turkey brigade. One damp morning, she handed me a canvas sack with a turkey inside and its head and shoulders showing. She told me to take the turkey to a cock on a farm at Coum a' Liaig, about four miles over Mount Eagle towards Ventry, through a passage known as Clasach, which had been cut into the mountain. Wearing our wellingtons, Páidín Kearney and I set off for the farm and took it in turns to carry the gobbling turkey under our arms. It was hard going, trying to hold on to the heavy turkey and climb the steep hill, which was waterlogged and muddy, as we had seen a lot of rain. Lo and behold, halfway up the hill, the turkey escaped and waddled off into the thick heather and furze. We raced after her in a panic, knowing we'd be for the slaughter if we went back home without her. Unfortunately, turkeys don't run in a straight line and we ran this way and that way, in and out in a zigzag, trying to catch her. Just as we caught sight of her, one of my wellingtons got stuck in the mud. Time was precious, so I left it behind me. We eventually caught up with the runaway turkey and stuffed her back into the sack. Páidín clutched her tightly while I trailed back in search of my abandoned wellington. By then we were plastered in muck from head to toe. Breathless, we plodded on as best we could. When we finally staggered into the farmyard, we were greeted by an enormous cock. The size of him scared the living daylights out of us, so much so that we opened the bag, flung the turkey at him and ran for our lives in the direction of the farmhouse, where we were treated to bread and jam and a mug of milk.

On 5 May 1959, when I was in sixth class, I got another new sister, Josephine. She was a big, bubbly, ten-pound baby and I quickly grew to love her. But for some reason or other that I fail to recall, by Christmas I became very clingy towards Mam. She decided I should go to the primary school in Dingle in January. I can't explain her decision, but I have no memory of being unhappy at school in Dunquin. Maybe Mam wanted me to be more independent, or maybe she thought if I went to Dingle I'd do better in my primary certificate exam, which was only a few months away, and improve my chances of getting a scholarship to a secondary school. Or maybe she had boarding school in mind for me and wanted me to get used to being away from home. Whatever her reason, moving to Dingle marked a huge turning point in my life. Looking back now, I see it as the end of my childhood.

Attending the primary school in Dingle was an eye-opener to me, a shock to the system. For the first time, I became aware of the different structures of life. I realised that we're not all the same and that although a group of children may be in the same place, their experience of it may differ, unlike in Dunquin, where I thought we were all on an equal par, with the same abilities (apart from the time I got a swelled head about being an altar boy).

We had about twenty-five pupils in our class in Dingle. Brother Hannon taught us. He was cane mad. I was lucky that I was good at my lessons, but my heart went out to anyone who struggled, as they got the brunt of his anger. He seemed to like me and trained me for a singing competition, in which I sang a ballad, '*Cuan Bhéal Inse*', also known as '*Amhrán na Leabhar*'. There were only two other competitors in my section: Tomás Ó Sé, an uncle of the well-known television presenter, Daithí, and Tomas Ó Catháin from Ballyferriter. I came last.

During my time in Dingle I stayed with Hannah Kearney, a cousin of my father, who was a childless widow and a sister-in-law to Muiris Ó Súilleabháin, the author of *Twenty Years A-Growing*. At the time,

Hannah's brother, Seán Fillí, who had been the postman on the Great Blasket, lived with her and worked at the local hospital. Hannah, a big, tall, blonde, fun-loving woman, was kind to me, but she was tough and loud too. When she barked, I ran.

Every Thursday night, I strolled with Hannah, her neighbour Mrs Garvey and her son Páidí to Dingle pier to look for free fish from the boatmen. We packed a big bag to the brim and then Páidí and I lugged the sack of fish between us until Hannah and Mrs Garvey took over and carried it the rest of the way home, up near the football pitch.

At times, I felt a little lonely living with Hannah. I was always glad to go home on Fridays with Timmy McCarthy, who used to deliver bread to Kruger. On a Sunday night Kruger often dropped me back to Dingle, or I went with Aunt Kate and her family if they were visiting us for the day.

As well as sitting the primary certificate that summer, I also made my confirmation, without any great fuss. Mam and I went by hackney to Ballyferriter church, as I was still registered in Dunquin parish. I wore a blue suit. Afterwards we called in to Paddy Ó Catháin, a cousin of Mary Pheats Mhicí, for a bite to eat. Then we headed home and changed straight away into our everyday clothes.

From then on, all the talk centred on which secondary school I should attend. At the time, we had a boy staying with us from Saint Munchin's College in

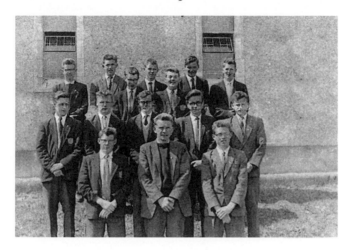

Sixth year students of Saint Joseph's College, Freshford,
County Kilkenny, in 1961. Breandán Ferriter is in the
back row, extreme left.

Limerick, which was well known for its success on the
field in rugby. When he showed me his rugby boots
and jersey, I was blown away, as they were so unlike my
football gear. The thought of getting new sports gear
in strong, vibrant, fresh colours appealed to me.

By then, Breandán Ferriter had been a boarder for
a few years at Saint Joseph's College in Freshford,
County Kilkenny, which was a secondary school run
by a missionary order, the Mill Hill fathers, and known
as Freshford. The college drew pupils from all over
Ireland, especially from Kerry. Upon finishing there,
many of the students entered the order's seminary in
Dublin, with the intention of becoming priests.

Like Kruger, Breandán was a great spin doctor. He could sell sand to the Arabs and he sold the college to me as if it was Hollywood, a holiday camp and Croke Park all in one. As well as that, two priests from the college, Father Hayes and Father O'Rourke, spent the summer in Dunquin at the house of Mary Pheats Mhicí's sister, Kate, the princess. Father O'Rourke was big into football and often took the Ferriters and myself down to the strand for a game of ball or away for spins in his car, with football always being the main topic of conversation. He popped in a lot to Mam and Dad too, for a chat and a cup of tea.

The summer holidays had barely started when I told Mam that I'd made up my mind about where I wanted to go. It had to be Freshford, nowhere else. Somewhere at the back of my mind, I fancied myself as a priest, like many youngsters in the village, who thought there was no better role in life. Freshford would be my starting point. Mam went along with my choice even though Freshford gave no scholarships, but I think she may have felt that Freshford might give me an advantage in life. Being familiar with all the academics who visited Dunquin, she would have seen education as the key to a big job and a good lifestyle. Or maybe Father O'Rourke had sold it to her as a ticket to success, just like Breandán had sold it to me.

Dunquin

On the day Breandán and I were loading our big suitcases into Kruger's van, ready to go to Dingle for the bus to Tralee, the postman Tom Johnson rode casually along on his bike, on his way from Ballyferriter, and said, 'Bejesus, Kruger, there'll be a lot of priests in this village yet!'

7

The Boarder

IN TRALEE, BREANDÁN and I lugged our heavy suitcases into the train station. On the platform, we bumped into a few lads who were also on their way to the college. I chatted to one of them, Tim Kelliher from Milltown, near Killarney, who was starting off like me. It marked the beginning of a close friendship. Years later, Tim became a household name when he played with the Kerry senior football team.

When the gang of us hopped on the train to Thurles, I felt as if I was heading off on a big adventure, as I'd never been on a train before and had never gone beyond Tralee. The train stopped at every station along the way. I was in no rush and lapped up every single second of the trip. I loved the way the train chugged along, making a rhythm all of its own, rocking everyone in their seats. Any time I spotted someone dozing, I nudged Breandán and nearly choked with laughter. I tuned in to all the natter around me, gazed excitedly out the window beside me, then switched to the one opposite, then back again. I feasted my eyes on all the sights along the way: houses with smoking chimneys, cattle grazing in the fields and fishermen wading knee deep in water. When anyone boarded, I looked them up and down and wondered where they might be going. If a young boy stepped on with a big suitcase, I decided he was surely heading for Freshford.

At Thurles we boarded a special bus laid on to carry students heading to Freshford from the south and west. It was dark when we landed, but the college was all lit up. A big cluster of tall stone buildings, bounded by vast grounds, it shone like a beacon in the night. The priests were lined up outside to greet us, among them Father Hayes and Father O'Rourke, who both shook hands with me.

All the first year students were led up a wide, winding marble staircase to the dormitory. As juniors, we were forbidden from having any more contact with the senior students. For me, that meant Breandán was out of bounds, as he was in fifth year. Each of us was given a bed with a locker beside it, into which we were told to fold our clothes neatly. After saying some prayers in the chapel, we were taken to the refectory, which was a massive hall, for supper. Then we were sent to bed and told to stay silent by Father Ryan, who had charge of night duties and the dormitories. He paced up and down the dormitory like a prison officer.

At 9.30 p.m. he switched off the lights. Minutes later, I heard a boy sobbing his heart out.

The next morning, I woke around six o'clock. Even though I was surrounded by about twenty-five other lads, I felt terrible – totally isolated and trapped. Although I had stayed with Hannah Kearney for months and was used to being away from home, there was no comparison, as I was now on the other side of the country, far away from Dunquin and cooped up with strangers in a rigid, enclosed, English-speaking, male environment with no home comforts and no touch of homeliness. I felt hemmed in, restrained, as if I was no longer the free spirit I had always been. I just did not fit in and thought I stuck out like a sore thumb. I even felt conscious about my name, as the name Gearóid was uncommon.

At 6.15 a.m., Pat Kennedy, a senior guy who had the task of waking us each morning, walked up and down the dormitory ringing a bell. Holding our towels and soap, we lined up at the sinks outside the dormitory and washed ourselves with cold water.

We marched downstairs along the corridor and into the church for meditation, followed by Mass at 6.45 a.m. Then we went back upstairs to tidy the dormitory before having breakfast in the refectory. A priest sat at the head of each table and passed down big plates of porridge. It was hard, lumpy and salty, unlike Mam's smooth, creamy porridge. Nuns did all the cooking in the kitchen, but they were kept out of sight at all times, just like the female secretaries. We ate in silence, which was the rule. If anyone dared speak, the head of the table rang a bell.

After breakfast, we washed our teeth and took a ten-minute walk in the grounds. I strolled with Tim. We went round and round in circles along the pathway. All the boys looked glum.

At 8.40 a.m. in the main hall, we sat an exam of Irish, English, maths, geography and history. All the tests were set in English. I sailed through the Irish paper, but found the maths questions tough. We were divided into classes based on the results. No allowance was made for the fact that some of us were not fluent in English. Any students who excelled went straight into second year, among them Tim Kelliher.

When class started, we were given our books for the year. Our curriculum was made up of Greek, Latin, French, science, physics and Christian doctrine as well as the subjects we had taken in the exam. We also got our sports gear of socks, shorts and jerseys, all in the sharp college colours of black and red, along with our ties, scarves, caps and blazers showing the college crest, '*Amare et servire*', which means 'to love and serve'. Every single item of clothing had to be tagged to make sure everyone got back all their garments every week from the laundry, which was also run by the nuns. They were totally reliable, as nothing ever went missing.

Classes started at 8.40 a.m. every morning and ended with prayers at 12.15 p.m., followed by lunch, then a ten-minute walk or free time. Classes ran again from 1.40 p.m. to 3.00 p.m., followed by an hour of sports, then tea and a walk in the grounds. Classes resumed at 4.45 p.m. and ran until 5.30 p.m., when we said prayers, followed by the Angelus in the church. Then we had supper and studied until 8 p.m. We spent the next hour in the library one week and in the games room the following week, playing table tennis, billiards, draughts or chess. By the time we hit the pillow each night, most of us were out for the count.

As the days went on I grew more and more disillusioned with the place, which failed miserably to live up to Breandán's glossy image. In class, I felt the other boys were way ahead and that I had learned next to nothing in primary school. I felt backward, frustrated and isolated. Not being fluent in English was a huge drawback, as I couldn't express myself well when the teachers asked me a question. It ruined my confidence. I felt like a fool, stammering and stuttering, trying to get out what I wanted to say, with teachers sneering at me and the whole class giggling. But the words would not come. I cursed my heritage for neglecting my education and tried to understand how it came to be that I could not speak English fluently even though I lived only about fourteen miles from Dingle. I felt that the gulf between me and the rest of the class was vast, but it must have been the same for all the boys from Irish-speaking areas, whether from Donegal or Galway. I thought about all the people from the Great Blasket who had emigrated and wondered how they coped. Not being fluent in English must have been a huge burden and must surely have isolated them and limited their chances of success.

The rule on silence got to me too, big time. The restriction of only being allowed to talk in the grounds or while playing games was too harsh, and breaking the rule could result in expulsion. I found the discipline of each and every minute of each and every day crippling.

On the tenth day, the loneliness came down on me like a ton of bricks. I'd had enough and wanted to go home. With the long winter nights about to set in, things could only get worse. I bawled my eyes out non-stop. I didn't give a hoot who heard me, unlike the broken-hearted boy in the dormitory who sobbed into his pillow every night but hid his emotions by day. Father Hayes had a chat with me. It did no good. Then Father Gillespie, the master of discipline, came along. I told him I couldn't take it anymore, that the rules were too severe and I needed my freedom. He tried to coax me to stay. I just did not want to know. Then Breandán was brought along to have a chat with me. We sat on a bench on the grounds. He told me it would get better, that he had felt the same when he started. I cried and cried and said I wanted to go home. I missed my family and I missed Dunquin, even though I knew that in winter the village was always deserted, pitch black, with no electricity, and silent, as the sound of passing cars and the laughter of tourists were only a distant memory. But I needed to go home.

The decision was taken to isolate me, maybe because I might upset the other boys, or maybe to help me snap out of it. I was put into a small room in the infirmary, which was an area set aside for ill students. My meals were brought up to me there. Most of the time I just slept. On the third day, I walked out of the room, picked up my football boots and shorts and headed for the pitch, where my classmates were playing a match between themselves. I joined in as if nothing had happened.

From then on, I got on with it. The thought of the challenge faced by emigrants from the Great Blasket spurred me on and I became adamant that I was not going to be a whipping boy for anybody. Instead, I would do my people proud.

Irish became my saving grace, as I excelled at it. In the long winter nights, I read books galore in the library, mainly from the Irish section. I raced way ahead of the class. Our Irish teacher, Mr McCarthy – a lovely, elderly man who lived in the lodge at the entrance – praised me to the hilt. That in itself boosted my confidence, restored my self-belief and helped me cope a little better with the other subjects. I joined the choir under Father Vijn and sang my heart out as a soprano. I became part of the dramatic society run by the dynamic Father Cannon, who was famous for putting on lively musicals, such as those by Gilbert and Sullivan. I sang in the chorus and everyone at home laughed their heads off when they saw a picture of me wearing a girl's costume. In one concert I sang '*An Madairín Rua*' on my own, even though I was scared out of my mind at the thought of standing on the stage alone and facing an audience, as the isolation of the Great Blasket had made me fearful of crowds.

I served as an altar boy too, as any new boy who had been an altar boy was asked to serve Mass each morning. Twelve priests celebrated Mass at the same time, one at each of the twelve side altars. The Mass was said in Latin, with no sermon. One priest, Father Morris, could say Mass in just over twelve minutes. We all wanted to serve his Mass to gain some extra free time.

I became an ardent player on the basketball team and ran around the court with zeal, dribbling the ball, passing it or aiming high for the net. I spent hours on the tennis courts and tried to perfect my serve, convinced I could win every game with a shower of aces. The college boasted four football pitches and I played left fullback on the football team, which was a mix of all counties, from Kerry up to Derry and down to Wexford. We laughed our heads off at all the different accents, as sometimes we couldn't understand each other. The Kerry boys became known as 'Pucks', the Dublin lads as 'Jackeens' and the townies as 'Teddy Boys'. I loved the *craic*, especially heading off on a bus to

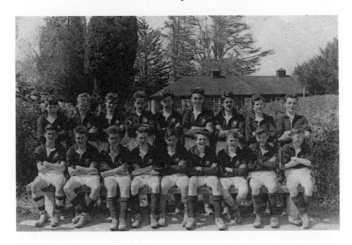

Juvenile football team, Saint Joseph's College, Freshford, County Kilkenny, in 1962. Gearóid is fourth from the left in the front row with Seán Ferriter (*third from left*) and Tim Kelliher (*fifth from left*) beside him. Both were close friends of Gearóid's. Author's own collection.

play other colleges in the inter-college championships, as we sang all the way, going and coming back, win or lose. Mam was shocked to read in my letters that I had played in Counties Laois, Wexford, Offaly and Tipperary, but they were all near, whereas to go from Dunquin to Cork or Limerick took a huge amount of travel. I played hurling too with the class team. We fought hard on the pitch to win, especially when we took on other classes, as the rivalry between the classes was huge. Father Todd, an English priest, had charge of sport. He was great fun, very spontaneous. On

Sundays, regardless of weather, all wrapped up in our overcoats, we set off on a twelve-mile walk, six miles over and six miles back, usually towards Tullaroan or Barna. The landscape was totally different to Dunquin, with flat, fertile land, an abundance of trees and no mountains. The air was crisper and colder, with little rain. Still, I missed the sea and even though I always trudged along on the Sunday walk with my best pals in the class – John Courtney from Killarney and William McHugh from Donegal – the long trek bored me to tears. And I hated wearing an overcoat, as it was heavy and too warm. Apart from passing away the day, the trek kept us off the pitches and gave the ground a chance. And with all the going, it was easy to work up an appetite.

On the whole, the food was top class, as the college ran its own farm, which was well stocked with cows, cattle and sheep. Every Sunday morning we ate a feed of sausages for breakfast. For some reason or other, mutton was dished up for lunch more often than any other meat. Many days we ate minced meat, which was unheard of at home. An abundance of fruit grew in the college's walled-in orchard, which gave us a great variety of desserts, such as stewed apple or gooseberry with custard. For evening tea we usually ate potatoes and a small stew. The food landed on the table in big dishes and was then divided out by the priest at the top of the table. Usually about six lay teachers and priests sat at each table with the students. Soon I became known as 'Savage', as I ate heartily and always cleared my plate.

At Hallowe'en we had great fun picking baskets of apples and gooseberries from the orchard. We lit a massive bonfire and sat around it, watching the flames rise higher and higher and singing along with Father Vijn as he strummed his guitar. He was a great guy, always jovial and humming to himself. I tucked into a parcel from home and stuffed myself with homemade barmbrack and my favourite sweets.

Every week Mam wrote me a letter in Irish, filled with news about my sisters and Dad and all the local gossip. I was always careful with my reply, as the superiors checked and censored letters before popping them in the post. Some boys who lived near the college were lucky enough to get visits from their parents, who usually took them off for a spin and a bite to eat.

When the results of the Christmas exam were posted on the notice board, we made an almighty racket pushing our way through to see our grades. Father Todd shouted out in his English accent, 'Quiet!' and the noise stopped instantly. I scored high marks in Irish, Latin, Greek and English. By then I had mastered the written word in English and improved my spoken English thanks to Father Cannon, who helped me along and built up my confidence. Thrilled to bits that I had done so well and that the term was over, I couldn't wait to go home for the holidays. All the boys felt the same. The excitement was unreal.

About two days before Christmas, dressed in our uniforms and overcoats, we boarded the bus to start the journey home. When Breandán and I landed in Dingle, Mam and Faeilí were already in the town, doing some Christmas shopping. They squeezed me so tight that I nearly broke in bits. They whisked Breandán and myself off to Joe Curran's shop, which was divided into a pub at one side and a saddlery and a clothes shop at the other. They treated us to a tall glass of lemonade and bombarded me with questions, one after another, wanting to know every detail of my time away. Breandán was well used to coming and going and he just folded his arms, sat back and smiled to himself at all the fuss.

When I walked in home, the smallness of the rooms and passages hit me. Before, I had thought of the place as a palace. Now it looked no bigger than a doll's house. I saw a huge change in my sisters, especially in Josephine, who was quickly moving on from the baby stage.

Then I spotted that most of my treasured cowboy comics and annuals were missing from the cupboard. Mam told me that Josephine had pulled them down by standing up on her pram and torn them asunder. I went into a terrible tantrum, but Mam kept the peace and in time I cooled off.

It was a magical Christmas, hanging around with my pals again and stuffing myself with Mam's home cooking. All the villagers showed great goodwill towards me and made me feel important. When I popped into Kruger's, he curtsied at the sight of me, just like he used to do upon seeing Siobhán McKenna. He roared at me that I had grown into the finest young man he had ever seen. Of course, it all went to my head and I became the greatest show-off in the village, especially on Christmas morning. I marched into the church for Mass wearing my college blazer, with my cap in my hand and my scarf swung casually over my shoulder. The priest said three Masses, all in Latin, one after the other. I attended all three to make sure everyone in the village saw me. My single regret was that I got only one chance to swagger all the way up to the altar to receive communion. But Pat and Seán Ferriter were every bit as bad as me. At the time, Pat was home on holiday from the seminary in Killarney and Seán was home from Farranferris in Cork and they paraded around the church in their college blazers as if they were on a catwalk in Paris.

When the Christmas holidays ended, I left to go back without any great fuss. Having survived the first three months and broken the back of it, I felt different, more mature, tougher, almost invincible. I looked forward to meeting the lads again and catching up on all their news.

When Saint Patrick's Day came, the college pulled out all the stops and celebrated in style. A white tablecloth adorned the dining tables and we got extra portions of food, along with jugs of orange juice and lemon juice drinks galore. We held our own provincial championships in both hurling and football, with each team representing one of the four provinces. Then on 19 March we celebrated Saint Joseph's Day, as the college was named in honour of Saint Joseph. We had a free day, which started off with concelebrated Mass on the main altar and ended with a film. The college always showed great films, such as *Boys Town*, which starred my favourite actor, Mickey Rooney. The film told the story of a priest working with disadvantaged and delinquent boys in a home he founded. Maybe I liked it so much because I could relate to it, being at boarding school. I loved westerns too, such as *The Sheepman*, and I became a huge fan of all the cowboy actors, like Glenn Ford, John Wayne, Audie Murphy and Alan Ladd.

The build-up to the summer holidays began in May. A big concelebrated Mass was said to pray for fine weather so that all the crops could be saved. The cutting of silage started on the college farm, unlike in west Kerry, where the farmers saved hay. The silage was heaped into a huge mound in the barn and each class was called in turn to stamp on it, wearing our football boots. It reeked of acid and stunk like buttermilk.

During the summer holidays of 1961, when I was fourteen years of age, I helped out a lot at home, especially during the month of June, when my father went shearing sheep on the Blaskets. Most days I set off with a donkey and cart to draw turf from An

Maoilinn and from Páirc Ghiarra. I took Josephine
and Ann Marie with me and the three of us sat in
the cart, which had wooden panels on both sides to
hold in the turf. I stacked the turf flat and built it up.
Sometimes I tied it down with rope. Usually I brought
home twenty loads a week. I dug potatoes and other
vegetables too and often helped to milk the cows. But
most of the time Mam liked to do the milking herself,
both morning and evening. I cooked big suppers for
Ann Marie and Josephine, mostly Irish stew, followed
by desserts, the recipes for which I would have taken
from Freshford.

Despite helping out at home, I found time for
some fun too. I played football every day with Páidín
Kearney, Seán Ferriter, Mairtin Beag, Donie Larry,
Tommy Mitchell and Mícheál Daly. We played in
our shorts and bare feet. Instead of kicking around a
football, we usually played with one of the basketballs
Breandán had brought home from Freshford. At the
end of each game we bathed our feet in the sea or
soaked them in iodine when we went home, as our
insteps were always red-raw from kicking the hard,
heavy, ribbed basketball. In every game, my main rival
was Páidín. I could never beat him, as I was too thin
and light, whereas he was solid and strong.

At night we plastered our hair with so much
Brylcreem that it ran into our ears and down our
necks. Then we hopped on our bikes and cycled to
the local *céilí*. The bikes came in handy, especially
for the older lads, as they could take their girlfriends

home on the handlebars. We used to cycle four abreast down the road near Gleann na Claise Móire. It was a dangerous stretch of road, with no ditch and a stream nearby. We often crashed into each other, as none of us had a bicycle lamp. Once, on the way home in the dark, Donie Larry hit a donkey when cycling around a corner and went head over heels into a field.

One night at the *céilí* we spotted an older, single guy, dressed in a snow white, see-through shirt, with hair oil flowing down his back. 'Look at the cut of your man,' Mairtin said. 'He's like something from a horror movie.' The gang of us got a fit of laughing and made a ferocious racket. The parish priest dashed over and warned us, 'If ye don't behave, ye are out of here.'

At the dances we always gave the local girls the cold shoulder, even though they fancied us like mad, especially those of us home from boarding school. We only had eyes for the teenage tourists. They looked more alluring than the girls from the parish, as they wore brighter colours and looked smarter.

On the morning after the *céilí* I was always out for the count, too tired to get out of bed. Dad had war. One morning he appeared at my bed waving a hatchet and roaring, 'If you're not out of that bed in two seconds, you'll get this over your head!' I had no choice but to get up, as I still served Mass every morning with Mairtin, Donie and Tommy. I still loved reading, but if Dad ever found me stuck in a book on a cock of hay, he quickly put the skids under me.

Group photograph of all the students of Saint Joseph's College, Freshford, County Kilkenny. Gearóid is in the front row, seventh from right.

When the summer holidays ended, I felt sick at the thought of leaving the house and dreaded going back to Freshford. I went only for the sake of sticking it out, even though I now had more company than ever, as Páidín Kearney and Seán Ferriter joined me and Breandán returned to enter his final year. Páidín started in first year. I went into third year, as I had done so well in my summer exams that I was allowed to skip second year. Seán had already spent a year at Farranferris and he went into the same class as me.

As the weeks went by, I noticed that Páidín never complained, although he must have felt lonely sometimes. Then again, maybe having me there had helped him to settle in, as we were both alike in many ways. He always gave me his mother's letters to read. She had beautiful handwriting and told all about the visitors to the house and the local characters. There was a certain poignancy about her letters and they made me feel lonely, unlike Mam's letters. Maybe Mam went out of her way to avoid painting a warm picture of home, as she would have known that it might upset me, having been away from home herself. Seán was always full of life and showed no signs of loneliness.

During the year, I kept up all the activities I had started in first year. As time went on, I grew braver and bolder. My favourite hobby became sliding down the long, polished corridor at speed, which was strictly against the rules. I often crashed into Father Gillespie, the master of discipline, a tall, lively guy whom all the juniors liked. He would simply smile and say, 'Keane, where is the Kerry train?'

But it wasn't all fun and games. For the first time in my life, I realised that the teaching of Irish must have gone astray in some form, as the boys from non-Irish-speaking areas didn't have a clue and lacked a basic understanding of the language. The sheer terror on their faces as they walked into the Irish class was disturbing, as they knew they were in for a beating if they failed to answer questions properly. First, those who gave a wrong answer were told to kneel behind the door of the classroom. Sometimes four or five boys might be kneeling down together. If they missed another question, they were marched right up to the rector of the college for a caning. My heart went out to those lads. Their suffering had a huge impact on me. Years later, when I gave grinds in Irish, I bent over backwards to help my students, as I never forgot the fear on the faces of my classmates. It affected me deeply. Even today, something stinks about how the Irish language is perceived. Leaving it to academia will kill it. We need a revival, someone with a fresh approach who could make the language appeal to the masses, someone like Seán Ó Riada, who brought traditional music out of the dark corners and bogs and showed it for what it was, brought it into concert halls and chambers and made it into a worldwide industry. Punishing those who cannot cope with the language serves no purpose and speaking a few words of Irish every day for the month of March in collaboration with RTÉ is merely a drop in the ocean and will not help revive the language. In the Irish class, I myself felt untouchable, immune from punishment, as I knew I wouldn't mess up. But I got my share of clattering in other classes, especially in the history class.

The priest who taught us history was a pompous ass who believed there was only one way of doing things. It had to be his way, bottom line. He taught us through a method of synopsis and showed us how to answer questions by listing points in a certain order. If any of us forgot a point or listed the points in the wrong order, he belted us. When I failed to grasp one particular lesson, he became highly insulted. It stuck in his craw. From then on, he was down on me. He took great pleasure in hitting me, maybe because I came from the Blaskets and was the son of a fisherman-farmer. If we felt we were being treated unfairly by a teacher we could complain to Father Gillespie, but we usually just put up with it.

During the summer holidays, in the middle of August, Breandán called to me at home on his way to Puck Fair, all excited. He said he had done well in his Leaving Certificate and had won a scholarship to University College Galway. Then out of the blue, Páidín and Seán told me that they would not be returning to Freshford. Instead, they were going to start at the secondary school in Dingle. My world fell apart. I felt gutted and hated the thought of heading back to Freshford alone. My only consolation was that I would be meeting up with my college pals again, but when I got back I found out that a few of them had dropped out too. Nonetheless, I got on with it and stuck it out until Christmas.

When I came home for the Christmas holidays, Páidín and Seán were on a high, telling all about the great fun they were having at school in Dingle and laughing about how laid back it all was in comparison to Freshford, with little or no discipline and no rules of silence. They were drawing me in, bit by bit, and I fell for it, just like I had fallen for Breandán's fine description of Freshford. I began to ask myself what I was doing staying in that prison. After Christmas, I told Mam I wanted to go to Dingle instead. She let me have my way without any great fuss.

In the New Year, I started in Dingle and settled in without a bother, as I had more freedom now and never felt confined in any way. Teaching was of the highest order. Brother Lennon, who taught us maths and Latin, put great emphasis on competition. He divided us into pairs and invented an imaginary trophy. The winning pair escaped study and home-work for a day. The rivalry was fierce. For added effect, some of my classmates started sprucing up their uniforms. We all ended up wearing flashy ties, mostly from parcels sent by our relatives in America, and Brother Lennon threw in a few extra marks for the most flamboyant ties.

Football took off big time for me and my team made it into the O'Sullivan Cup, which was a first for the school since 1938. The lads and myself were now cock of the walk, convinced we were the best footballers to come out of Dingle for decades, and we swaggered around the place, full of our own importance. Our team was made up of Tomás Keane, Seán Ferriter, Tommy O'Dowd, Paudie Garvey, Muiris MacDonald, Thomas O'Connor, Tomaisín Sé, John Martin, Pól Scanlon, Paudie McKenna, Mícheál Ó Laoithe, Tomaisín Ó Cíobháin, Páidín Ó Cearna and Tom Fitzgerald. Brother Smith and Mr Costelloe trained us, while Brother Lennon held the purse strings for our away trips. Our most avid supporter was Ger Fox. Twice we drew against Abbeyfeale secondary school. In the third match against them we were heading for another draw, then I scored two goals. That finished them off.

In the final of the Kerry colleges B division, we played against Cahirciveen CBS. They were bigger and stronger than us. I was put into centre field to mark the massive Kerry minor, Pat O'Connell, who was over six feet tall. Any time I jumped for the ball, I came no higher than his shoulder. Not long into the game, I pulled a hamstring. Nobody paid any attention to it so I played on. Together, we suffered and battled on to the bitter end, but we were no match for Cahirciveen. They destroyed us.

Luckily, we had other interests apart from football, namely the girls in the local secondary school. Over time, the abandoned cars outside Cleary's garage in Dingle became a favourite haunt for us and many a romance blossomed there.

Yet despite the distractions in Dingle, I never got a bad school report and did very well in my Leaving Certificate, although looking back later, I felt I may have done even better if I had stayed at boarding school. The time had come for me to choose my career path. Brother Lennon advised me to become a primary school teacher, but by then I'd had my fill of school life. I opted for a different route.

On the day before I left Dunquin to start full-time work, I sat beside my father in a field as he was setting spuds and we talked. He kept his pipe in his mouth and muttered a few words every now and then. He was a quiet man by nature, who never used control and rarely raised his voice. Yet you knew he was there. I often wondered how he felt about the fact that I had spent so many years away from home, but he never told me. Now I was leaving again. Out of the blue in the field that day he said to me, 'It's best that you leave this place. Your future is not on the land. And anyway, won't you finish your day's work early? Here, it never ends.' This was extraordinary. I had never stopped to think about all he had to do. He was always going somewhere – to the bog, to shear sheep, to fish, to till and sow, to take tourists to the Blasket Islands, to go to Brú na Gráige to play music at the *céilí* and to give haircuts. He was all over the place, day and night, doing a variety of work. And here I was, about to take on only one job.

Now, looking back, maybe I regret that I didn't stay and work beside him to learn how to give haircuts, play the fiddle or spend a week or two on the islands shearing sheep. Maybe he saw the futility of that life, the sheer intensity of battling constantly against the elements and having little or nothing to show for it at the end of the day. Young and enthusiastic, I had set my own priorities. A life on the land was not for me and I think he saw that. My half-hearted attempts at rural work were not encouraging and may have been short lived. Emigration might have been on the cards. Above all else, I think my time out of the village at boarding school had mapped out my future. That was it.

8

A Visitor from the Past

THE PAST CAN CREEP up on us when we least expect it, as happened to me some years after I moved to Cork.

When I finished my Leaving Certificate I started work as a shop assistant with MacGearailt & Co., which was based in the Grand Parade in Cork. At the time, the firm was the biggest electrical contracting company in the south of Ireland, with clients such as University College Cork on its books as well as most hotels in Cork city and county. My boss was Séamus MacGearailt from Cobh, who was chairman of the Harbour Commissioners. He had an interesting past, as he had served as a member of the first Dáil and had been interned during the Irish civil war. Over time I moved from the shop into the office, and on Seamus' recommendation I studied accountancy by night at the School of Commerce. When I moved into digs in the

Marie and Gearóid at their first dinner dance together in
the Metropole Hotel, Cork, in the late 1960s.

Ballinlough area of the city with a kind woman named
Mrs O'Sullivan, I joined the local GAA club, Nemo
Rangers. I made some great friends there, among them

Brian Murphy, who later became regarded as the most successful GAA dual player of all time. And I was lucky enough to be part of the football teams of 1967 and 1968, when we won two city championships.

Dancing took up much of my time too, with the Arcadia ballroom being a favourite of mine. I usually went on a Wednesday night, which for some reason or other was called the dinosaurs' night. It was like a cattle mart, with the girls lined up at one side of the hall and the guys racing across the dance floor and pushing in droves to ask them to dance. If a girl agreed to dance, she usually stayed on for three dances. When the band called the next dance, the guy either asked her to stay on or let her go.

One night I was strolling around the back of the ballroom on my own when I heard the band announce the next dance. As I rushed to join in the shove, I spotted a beautiful, dark-haired girl wearing a pretty pink dress. I asked her to dance and we danced together for the rest of the night. Her name was Marie and I was smitten not only with her good looks, but also with her politeness. I made a date with her to go to the pictures on the following Saturday night. I waved her off as she hopped on the bus home to Bishopstown, on the edge of the city.

At Easter, when I took Marie home to Dunquin for the first time, we popped in to my cousin Mártan. He winked at me and told me to take Marie around Slea Head for a spin on his three-quarter-horsepower

Marie and Gearóid outside Saint Saviour's Church,
Dominick Street, Dublin, on 26 August 1972, their
wedding day.

motor bike. I whisked her off at full speed around the
narrow, winding cliff road and skimmed low around
the sharp bends. The elevation and speed got to Marie

and she could take no more. We ended up walking most of the way back to Mártan's house and Marie vowed to never, ever again get up on a motorbike. She kept her promise.

Back in Cork, I got big into bikes. I bought a Honda one-and-a-half, which was a powerful machine. Noel O'Halloran, a buddy of mine at work, was obsessed with bikes too. Whenever we got the chance the two of us would hit the road and ride away to bike scrambles all over the country.

Marie and I married in Dublin in 1972. It was the first time our families had met. We held our wedding reception in the Intercontinental Hotel. Mam's only concern was trying to persuade my father to leave off his cap, as he always wore it, no matter what, except when he sat down to eat. Before the wedding she sent him off for a haircut. He came back looking like a new man, years younger, as the barber had given him a smart trim and put a slight colour in his hair. On the day of the wedding he annoyed my mother to no end, looking for his cap every minute and asking, 'Can I put it on now?' But she held tough and kept it hidden away in her handbag. As the night went on, he forgot about it and gave us all a good knees-up by playing the fiddle.

After five years at MacGearailt & Co. I moved to Marina Bakery, which was a subsidiary of Ranks Ireland. I stayed there until 1983, when I was made redundant along with 325 others. From then on I

Gearóid's son Graham and daughter Sandra taken at home
in the mid-1990s.

worked for a number of other companies, mainly in
the financial departments, but years later I changed
course and worked with FÁS as a supervisor.

Marie and I were blessed with two children, Sandra
and Graham. When Sandra was small I often took
her to matches at Páirc Uí Chaoimh, which was only
down the road from where we lived. We'd stop off at a
shop on the way and stuff our pockets with sweets. At

half time, when all the sweets would be gone, Sandra would demand to go home. Graham and I were always close too, more like friends than father and son.

Although I was happily settled in Cork, the Blasket Islands were never far from my thoughts. During the 1970s an American named Taylor Collings, who had moved to the Dingle Peninsula in the early 1970s, began calling to the homes of the islanders, asking them to sell their rights of the Great Blasket. He called often to our house in Dunquin and brought gifts. My father was tempted to sell, for the meagre sum of £100. I advised him against it and he held onto his rights. Most of the other islanders sold their houses on the island, their freehold rights to their land there and their commonage rights.

In 1985 the Blasket Island Foundation was formed to stop the sale of the Great Blasket and raise funds after a notice appeared in *The Wall Street Journal* saying the island was for sale. I became a member of the foundation, and in 1987, when *The Gay Byrne Show* asked for a spokesperson from the organisation to be interviewed on radio about the situation, I was sent along.

As I walked down the long corridor of the RTÉ studios in Donnybrook, I spotted Mike Murphy lounging at the door of an office with a big grin on his face, as if to say 'another one for the slaughter'. I suddenly began to feel uneasy at the thought of being interviewed by the great Gaybo, for whom I had huge

(*L-r*): Máirtín Tom Sheáinín Mac Donncha, Gearóid's
wife Marie and Gearóid at TG4 in June 2011 prior to
Gearóid's appearance on the programme *Comhrá*.

respect as a broadcaster. But I composed myself, as I
felt certain that the interview would last only a few
minutes. I also wanted to make my family proud, as
well as everyone connected with the Great Blasket,
and do all I could to save the island.

Gay was great and put me at ease straight away. None
can compare to him. He made me feel comfortable
and chatted away to me between the advertisements.
An hour later I was still on air with him as the phone
calls kept pouring in from people wanting to know
all about life on the Great Blasket. My aunt Nóiní in

Dublin phoned, just to say hello. And when I spoke about the fact that I love being alone, in isolation, one listener rang in to say, 'That's called island madness!'

Thankfully, the Blasket Island Foundation stopped the sale of the Great Blasket and successfully campaigned for the island to be made an Irish National Park. They did great work and I often felt sad that I was unable to be more involved in the cause at the time. Stopping the sale from going ahead reminded me of the fact that the Americans who had wanted to adopt me when I was a child had failed to do so. As someone once said to me, 'You cannot buy culture.' Over time, the islanders learned that the island holdings of Taylor Collings had, in fact, been passed on to a group known as An Blascaod Mór Teoranta, which was led by a Dingle solicitor, Peter Callery, and his brother James.

Some days after being interviewed by Gay, I got the surprise of my life when I picked up the phone at home and a voice at the other end said, 'Hello, Gearóid. You won't remember me. My name is Liam Robinson. I'm the journalist who wrote the article about you, the loneliest boy in the world, way back in the late 1940s.' My heart skipped a beat. He went on to explain that he had been driving along a motorway in England when he happened to hear my interview with Gay Byrne and decided to contact me. We agreed to meet up soon after.

Liam came to Cork by train and we spent the day at the Ferryboat Inn, a popular pub on the Lower

Glanmire Road. I warmed to him straight away. He was nicely spoken, of medium build and had reddish hair. When he saw me, he tossed my hair and said, 'You have never changed, Gearóid. You still have a head of curls, just like you had when I last saw you.' We both laughed.

Liam spent most of the time reminiscing, recalling how he had stood on the harbour at Dunquin on Christmas Eve 1948 and looked across in terror at the high, rolling tide on which he was about to sail, with the sea thrashing hard against the rocks at the bottom of the cliff. He had fond memories of being fed lobster and conor by the islanders, with spuds and salt and a drop of hard liquor to wash it all down. He recalled that the islanders told him about a great hurling match that took place one Christmas on the island strand. The whole village took part and played with hurleys that were cut in Ventry. For a full week after, when they tried to walk up and down the hill to lead a cow home for milking, all their joints creaked and groaned like a rusty axle on a cart. He told me that what had astounded him most about his three-day trip to the Great Blasket was the sheer wilderness of the island. Later I took him home to meet Marie, as he had brought her a gift and wanted to give it to her in person.

When we shook hands and parted at the train station that evening, we promised to meet again. I had rarely thought about the impact of his article over the years, except when I was asked about it during interviews. But as I watched him walk along the platform to board the train, its importance hit me all of a sudden. How different would my life have been if Liam Robinson had never set foot on the Great Blasket and had never written that feature?

I left the station deep in thought, my mind filled with memories of toy trucks and trains, Roy Rogers, Davy Crockett and Wild Bill Hickok.

9

Partings

MY FATHER DIED SUDDENLY of a massive heart attack while staying with us in Cork for a few days. He came at the end of January, having taken a lift from Dunquin. We had planned a train trip to Dublin during his stay to meet Charles Haughey, who had invited us to his home, Abbeville, as he wanted to buy Inis Tuaisceart and needed to find out about the deeds.

Dad seemed fine when he arrived at our house on the Blackrock Road and the next night I took him for a drink to the Briar Rose with a friend of mine, Joe Downey. Early the following morning, Marie called me and said Dad was unwell. I rushed to his bedroom and found him crouched on the floor, on his knees. 'I'm dying, Gearóid,' he said. I lifted him onto the bed and ran down the road for a doctor. By the time I got back minutes later, he had passed away.

I needed to get the news to my mother and sisters, who were both at boarding school in Dingle. I rang an operator in Cork, who put me through to an operator in Killarney. I was then put on to an operator in Ballyferriter. At last I got through to Kruger's and spoke to Kruger's nephew, Paudie O'Neill. I told him that Seán Cheaist was dead and asked him to bring Faeilí to the phone.

Mam coped well with the news, maybe because she had been expecting it for a long time, as Dad had been a diabetic all his life and she had often seen him at death's door. When I lived in Dunquin, she had called me many times in the early hours of the morning and said, 'Get up quick, Gearóid. Your father is dying.' Whenever Dad went fishing, Mam would kneel and pray that he would not get a seizure while rowing at sea. When he went digging spuds he always took his time, but Mam often panicked if he was slow to come home and would say, 'He must have died.'

When my sisters finished boarding school, Ann Marie went nursing to Waterford and Josephine moved to Cork, then emigrated to Iceland and later to America. She seemed to have the travel bug, just like my aunt Nellie, to whom Mam used to send locks of my curls as a keepsake when I was a child.

Mam stayed on in Dunquin. Her neighbours were good to her, especially Mike Mitchell, a relation of ours. He always made sure that she had a supply of fresh milk, straight from the cow, and always had the

One man and his pipe – Gearóid's father going to the
Great Blasket in the late 1960s.

fire lighting for her when she came back from a visit to
me or to her sisters, Kate or Lís. Any time she stayed
with me, she always bought a bottle of whiskey for
Mike. She would work herself into a frenzy trying to
make up her mind about which brand to take, as she
was thankful for his help and wanted only the best for

him. Her constant companion became her widowed sister, Kate. They visited each other often, for a few days at a time, and dined together in Dingle once a week.

On her eightieth birthday she was still full of vigour. We held a surprise dinner for her at Tigh Pheig in Ballyferriter and I had her birthday called out on the local radio. She was not at all pleased with that and became cranky with me, maybe because she wanted to keep her age to herself. Still, she enjoyed the party, surrounded by her friends and close family, among them her nieces and her sister Kate.

In the late 1990s, while I was on holiday in Dunquin, I said to Mam that we should give the house a spring clean, a bit of a face lift. I forgot all about it until Ann Marie rang me at home some weeks later to say, 'You'll never guess what Mam is doing. She's dragging a table around the house and painting the ceilings.'

Soon after, on the day before my sister Josephine was due home from America on holiday, Mam took down the old curtains. A neighbour had promised to hang the new ones, but Mam became impatient waiting for her, climbed up on a chair, fell and broke her hip.

A few days before her operation, her sister Kate went into a coma and died. Mam missed her terribly and went downhill after her death. She lived for another seven years, but her zest for life had long gone.

In the autumn of 2004, just as the leaves were set to change colour, we laid her to rest on a dry day beside my father and his father, Ceaist, in An Teampall Nua, the new graveyard in Dunquin, facing the Blasket Islands. After the last prayers, Feargal MacAmhlaoibh, a local fiddler, played the familiar lament '*Port na bPúcaí*', which my father and grandfather used to play. Its haunting strains rose high above the hilly cemetery and swept me back in time, across the rolling waves to our home on the Great Blasket. There, I saw my mother and father together again, sharing a cigarette and reading the newspaper on the kitchen table. My mother twirled gaily around in a new floral dress, smiled at my father and asked, 'Well, Seán, what do you think?'

10

The Legacy

TODAY, THE IRISH STATE owns about two-thirds of the Blasket Islands, which consists of over one thousand acres. Under the Great Blasket Island Management Group, many agencies, such as the Heritage Organisations, Kerry County Council and the Department of the Marine, all work together to maintain the island and plan its future. Each year the Blasket Islands attract around twenty thousand visitors. Sometimes tourists hang around the mainland for days on end, looking out to sea and waiting to cross over, as the weather always dictates when they come or go. Even when the sun shines, the sea can be choppy and too rough for the ferries to sail to the islands.

Whenever I return to the Great Blasket, it pains me to stand on the slipway, knowing that I am the only survivor of all those who were evacuated from the island in 1953. They are all gone now, each and every

The Great Blasket village pictured many years after the evacuation of the island. Gearóid's house is on the right.
Courtesy of Críostóir Mac Cárthaigh.

one of them; Peaidí Mhicil was the last to pass away. An ancient, noble, island civilisation has been wiped out, utterly and completely.

As I climb the rocky pathway known as Bóithrín na Marbh, I try to picture the scene when my mother carried me up there as a newborn baby with all the islanders trailing behind, forming a procession and making their way to our home to toast my arrival.

Apart from holiday times, when the tourists came, it must have been a lonely, depressing life for them, especially in winter, when a thick, dreary mist hung over the island and darkness fell early. They must have been made of steel to cope with the great gales, when they had to close their doors for days on end, or to suffer illness without a doctor at hand. For the elderly especially it was a hard life, striving daily against the steep hill to cut turf and tend to their animals, always pulling and dragging and battling against the elements, with the island exposed on three sides and often battered by heavy rain and violent storms.

Walking into the field on the left of the pathway, I pause and look at our house. It breaks my heart to remember how it once looked, with its whitewashed walls, fine porch and felted, tarred roof. Now it stands as a cold, deserted shell with no roof, windows or doors and grass growing up through its centre, silent except for the mournful cry of a low-flying curlew, the clatter of the thrashing waves and the wail of the howling wind.

Yet when I go inside, I feel its warmth, as happy memories never fade. I see my grandmother, June Eoghain Bháin, with a small shawl over her shoulders, knitting woollen socks by the fire and beaming at my playacting. 'Who are you today, Gearóid?' she asks. And then Seán Fillí trudges across from the post office, laden down with a sack full of letters, postcards and parcels of clothes, books, comics and toys. He laughs and says to my mother, 'More of the same, Bídí.'

Islanders and mainlanders amongst the ruins of the village
in 1972 (*l–r*): Seánín Mhicil, Willie Devin de Mórdha,
Maras Mhaidhc Léan (hidden), Seán Pheats Tom Kearney,
Faeilí and Páidín Ó Catháin. Courtesy of Pat Langan.

When I go outside again and walk through the
abandoned village, from Bun a' Bhaile up to Barr
a' Bhaile, I see that most of the houses are like ours,
forlorn and crumbling. Some have been done up by
An Blascaod Mór Teoranta, like Tiúit's house, and

a house by the old school, which was turned into a café. I recall strolling up the village with Mam to visit my grandparents, Maras Mhuiris and Kate Sheáin Mhichíl, and my uncles, Faeilí and Maraisín Mhuiris. I think of the other villagers too, all of whom I loved – people such as Mary Pheats Mhicí, who always had a warm welcome for me; the great musician and fiddle-maker Seánín Mhicil; and Tom Pheaidí Mharas Ó Dálaigh, who could carve me a model trawler in the blink of an eye.

I come to the derelict outhouses where I used to stand with my grandfather Maras Mhuiris to watch the men rounding up the sheep. I remember it well, as if it happened only yesterday. But, most of all, I remember Christmastime, when my grandfather Ceaist and I would hurry down to the quay, hand-in-hand, to greet Mam coming home with all the Christmas fare. And I picture the beauty of the village on Christmas Eve, with a candle twinkling in every window, the frosted felt roofs shimmering like crystal and a full moon gleaming over Dunmore Head, illuminating the channel to the Blaskets.

When I remember Christmas on the Great Blasket, I think of Tiúit chatting by the fire to my grandfather Ceaist. Tiúit was never stuck for words and always had a string of questions on the tip of his tongue. One night he happened to ask my grandfather why our family had grazing rights on Inis Tuaisceart. My grandmother settled her shawl around her shoulders and Dad piled some more turf on the fire while Mam made a fresh pot of tea. I sat on her lap and snuggled into her as Ceaist took a puff of his pipe and began his story with Sheridan sound asleep at his feet.

'Well, Tiúit, my grandfather's name was Muiris Ó Catháin. He was born on Inis Tuaisceart in the 1830s and it is because of his family's ties with the island that our family has grazing rights there. Later, Muiris became known as Muiris na Tinte because he started married life in a tent in Dunquin. But a terrible tragedy happened to the family when Muiris was a child on Inis Tuaisceart and I will tell you about that now.

'On 14 June 1838, an antiquary from Cork named John Windele and other Corkonians, along with Father John Casey, the parish priest of Ballyferriter, sailed from Dunquin to Inis Tuaisceart. There, they found Muiris, his mother Peig, his father Tómás – who was my great-grandfather – and at least seven more of their children living in a cave, about eleven feet in diameter. Its roof was made of over-laying flags and had a small hole to let out smoke. Most of the children had been born and reared in the cave, where the family had lived alone for at least twelve years. Windele described Peig as being bare and elastic of foot.

'On the day of the visit, Tómás was not there, as he had rowed over to Dunquin. His wife welcomed the visitors and asked one of her sons to kill a rabbit or two for them, but they declined her kind offer. As the group were about to leave, she gave them a live stormie petrel, a delicacy much loved by the people of the Blasket Islands.

'Some years later, bad weather cut off the family from the mainland for six weeks, during which time Tómás died. Being too weak to move him out of the cave and unable to bear the stench, Peig began to dismember his putrefied body and throw pieces out through the smoke hole.

'When the weather improved and neighbours from the Great Blasket made their way to Inis Tuaisceart, they found Peig in a demented state in the cave, with the half-dismembered remains of her husband beside her. And so, Tiúit, our family's links with Inis Tuaisceart go way back to that sad time.'

After ending his story, my grandfather tipped back his cap, chewed his tobacco and waited for Tiúit's reaction. By then I was tired and Mam packed me off to bed. She tucked me in tightly and I cuddled up close to my teddy. I began to doze off, with strains of '*Port na bPúcaí*' drifting in from the kitchen and my head full of images of the cave.

Acknowledgements

PATRICIA AHERN

From the bottom of my heart, I want to thank Gearóid for his generosity in sharing his life story with us all and for giving me the great privilege of hearing his recollections first hand as well as the huge honour of co-writing the book. Working with Gearóid was a pleasure. Like his uncle Faeilí, he has a wonderful sense of fun and brings joy and laughter to everyone he meets. His story is indeed unique and truly deserves documentation. *Go raibh míle maith agat a Ghearóid.*

Thanks also to Gearóid's wife Marie for all the time and effort spent on locating research documents and photographs and for her warmth and hospitality always.

Thanks to The Collins Press. Many thanks also to Mairéad Ní Chonghaile of TG4 for introducing me to Gearóid after I contacted her following Gearóid's appearance as a guest on the television programme *Comhrá*. Thanks too to Fiona Crowe for the beautiful foreword, to freelance editor Kristen Jensen and to my sister Mary Lenihan for proofreading the text, for her recommendations and for her enthusiasm.

Thanks to everyone who helped with the research, especially Ríonach Uí Ógáin, UCD; Stiofáin Newman, Mary Immaculate College, Limerick; Seán Ó Laoi, UCC; and John Glendon, RTÉ.

Many thanks too to everyone who helped with the photographs, especially Dáithí de Mórdha, the Blascaod Centre, who was more than generous with his time and who provided us with a beautiful array of pictures.

Thanks for copyright permission to use photographs to the Blasket Centre; Don MacMonagle, MacMonagle Photography; the National Library of Ireland; the National Folklore Collection, UCD; the *Irish Examiner;* Liam Blake; Críostóir Mac Cárthaigh, UCD; Stan Mason; Pat Langan; and Maria Simonds-Gooding.

Many thanks also to my sister Joan Newman for her interest and encouragement and to the rest of my treasured family for their love and support always and for bringing a special sparkle to my life: my daughter Fiona; my sons Michael and Brian; my daughter-in-law Cathy; and my husband and best friend Denis.

Finally, thanks to Sister Ita of Saint Mary's Secondary School Mallow – the best, nicest and most hardworking teacher I ever had – for instilling in me many moons ago an abiding affection and deep admiration for the people of the Great Blasket through her wonderful teaching of *Peig.*

Thank you all.

Acknowledgements

GEARÓID CHEAIST Ó CATHÁIN

Many thanks to Micheál de Mórdha and Dáithí de Mórdha for their generosity in supplying photographs. They were generous to a fault and very patient and understanding. I had never seen some of the photos. *Go meadaí Dia bhúr stór.*

To Patricia, for having the idea of writing this story. When she approached me initially I hesitated, and as we sat down to talk I informed her that it would take only half an hour. She disagreed. I was glad she showed such enthusiasm as she guided me along and her sheer determination gave me the energy to continue. Sometimes, unbeknownst to her, I experienced extreme sadness when recounting certain chapters and many times I promised myself that her next visit would be the last and that we would abort the effort. She did not know this, of course, which was just as well. She knows now. I do not know how to thank her. She was absolutely marvellous. Her endurance, her courage and most of all, her kindness will always live with my family. She has a special place in our hearts.

Many thanks to Fiona Crowe for her wonderful foreword. To Don MacMonagle for his photos. To Pól Ruiséal, Seán Ó Laoi, Marian Ni Shúilleabháin, Clare Ni Mhuirthile, Nuala de Burca and Cearbhaill Ó Colmáin in Ionad Na Gaeilge Labhartha in University College Cork for their great support and encouragement. To Donie Butler for the marvellous pictures from Saint Joseph's College, Freshford.

He brings back fond memories. To Gearóid Ó Laoí and Pádraig Kennelly also for wonderful photos. To Diarmuid Ó Drisceóil for his great help in interpreting various documents. To my two sisters Josephine and Áine, who are continuing our family's music tradition. To Gael-Taca for their continuing support, most especially Pádraig Hamilton who, when we meet, brings me back to the days of old with his great tales of some of the people mentioned in my story. Many thanks also to The Collins Press for taking the initiative to publish the effort. *Go mbeannai Dia sibh go léir.*

To my grandfather Ceaist – Pádraig Ó Catháin – a big, strong man who battled many a squall. He was my constant companion in the very early years, a great piggy-backer when the road grew too long or when the waves grew too tall. To my grandmother June Eoghain Bháin, a woman of great stature and beauty, who was gentle and loving as I sat on her lap, with her arms extended and those knitting needles moving at speed and me watching her every twist and turn, and of course those great lullabies at bedtime.

To my grandfather Maras Mhuiris Ó Catháin, with those weather-beaten features, the big moustache and the great cane with its crook that dragged me to him when I was mischievous to wrap his arms around me in roguery. He was fond of strong tea – you could walk across the diameter of his mug. To my grandmother Kate Sheáin Mhichíl for her industry, tidiness and cleanliness, but most of all for her endurance. In the fishing season she washed Maras Mhuiris's clothes and dried them by the fire by staying up all night. 'Yerra,' she'd say, 'how could you send him out with his clothes full of salt water to do his day's work?' Now that was a woman.

To my father, Seán Cheaist. He was very handsome – loved by many women, I would say. He was very gifted: a fiddle player, a melodeon player, a carpenter, a shoemaker, a barber and a big rogue. Very quiet, gentle, not much to say, but according to folklore, very amusing and quick witted. To my mother, Bídí Mharas Mhuiris. She was very beautiful – paint, pearls and powder when travelling on occasions. A great cook, spotless and a great bread maker. She introduced my palate to the very extremes of its sensitivity. She was loving, kind and generous.

I miss them all. Their likes will never be again.

To my current family – to my wife Marie of forty years. What a team we make. Amidst upheavals and calm waters, we have stuck together. I impatient, chomping at the bit, she calm and patient. My rock. *Ná leaga Dia thú.* To Sandra, my first born. 'Those blue eyes,' said Marie when she was born. Beautiful, talented, extremely generous and happily married to Dónal, she embodies all the attributes of the Blasket women. To Graham, my son. The same mould as his father, mischievous, great endurance, athletic and most of all kind, considerate and a great husband to Erin and father to Seán Óg Cheaist. Sadly, he emigrated like my ancestors.

To Muintir an 'Leáin. What can I say about them? They were my teachers, coaches, fathers, mothers and many more. I sometimes regret that I did not stay young and they stayed the same. But time marches on and you sometimes wonder why. Would it be better if it moved and changed every hundred years? They would still be with me. Sadly, due to circumstances, I was unable to be with most of them on their deathbed. I cannot harness the wind or calm the sea. They are all in God's bosom, free from all toil and strife. They deserve it.

'These gentle souls no longer teach or toil,
Their ruins all that remain.
The barren slopes no more welcome their deeds,
All are gone just like the evening breeze.'

– Anon.

Index

NOTE: illustrations are indicated by page numbers in **bold**.

Index

Index

Index